Households of God

David Parry, OSB

HOUSEHOLDS OF GOD

The Rule of St Benedict with Explanations for Monks and Lay-people Today

Darton, Longman & Todd
London

First published in Great Britain in 1980
by Darton, Longman & Todd Ltd
89 Lillie Road, London SW6 1UD

ISBN 0 232 51461 5

Printed in Great Britain by the Anchor Press Ltd
and bound by Wm Brendon & Son Ltd,
both of Tiptree, Essex

I am writing these instructions to you, so that . . . you may know how to behave in the household of God.

I Tim 3:14–15 (RSV)

. . . so that no one may be upset or saddened in the household of God.

Rule of St Benedict (Ch. 31)

Preface

For one reason or another dissatisfaction with the quality of modern life is a common enough phenomenon today. That our modern world provides us with great benefits for which we should be grateful, no one can doubt. Indeed those parts of the world which have not received their full share of these benefits are often called 'under-developed', and in general they want to catch up with the more modern parts. And there is a strong feeling that we owe it to them to help them to do so. But the benefits in question seem to be mainly material, and the society which has been so successful in producing them is ill at ease in itself. The young and the not-so-young are often engaged in a hunt for that immaterial philosophy or religion which will satisfy the heart, and for a society knitted together by spiritual stitches, and not merely by physical or material bonds. Medical science is more and more aware that often the reasons why we are sick are not physical; the body is ailing because of a condition of the soul. Two things stand out as objects of permanent desire: the Transcendent (How do I find the answer to my soul's desires for the Other?), and the Community (How do we live together in love?).

It is surely a sad and sobering thing that many turn to the ancient religions of the East, because they do not think that Christianity meets these needs. The renewal of the Christian Churches has among its objects to show clearly that in fact Christianity does contain the most wonderful answers of all.

The need is to show, and not to the intellect only,

that in Christ the Word of God, the Transcendent One, became man, so that being one of us he might form us into a true community of human beings, transformed by his divine power into a family worthy of God. From this it follows that all Christianity is properly concerned with these two things: the return to God and the formation of a society such as to lead to that end. These things are not easy; they never have been easy, but they remain the unchangeable needs of man.

It was the very difficulty of fulfilling these things on the grand scale that gave birth to monasticism. However, the urge that led men into the formation of a kind of alternative society was not thought out just in those terms.

From the earliest times there existed in Christian Society persons known as ascetics or virgins whose zeal for the fulfilment of the Gospel was recognised as calling for a somewhat specialised life-style. There were communities too. In the Catacombs of St Priscilla a third-century fresco shows the Bishop giving the veil to some virgins. The realisation that Christ would not return as quickly as an earlier generation had thought led to an inevitable taking of new attitudes in the face of a society that was evidently going to continue.

A movement of enormous importance in the history of the Church began when one Antony, about the year AD 270, sold his considerable possessions, and retired into the Egyptian desert to seek intimacy with God in solitude and prayer. He was motivated by the Gospel text (which he had heard being read aloud in church), '*If you would be perfect, go sell all that you have, and give it to the poor, and follow me.*' He did not think in terms of community, but his example proved infectious.

Thousands followed him. Organisation inevitably ensued. In the fourth century in Egypt there were monasteries the size of villages or small towns.

Moreover, the difficulties of the undertaking, and the very real dangers of going astray, indicated the advantages of living together in community. Indeed to live in some kind of community is the natural condition of man. Christ himself had made use of this fact, and lived in community with his Apostles; and the first Christians are shown in the Acts of the Apostles as an intimate and loving community. These examples lived on in men's minds; so monastic life developed mainly on 'cenobitic' or communal lines.

From Egypt monasticism spread throughout the East; it also spread north to Europe. One of the most influential monks who brought the idea to Europe was John Cassian (c. 360–436). He had lived some fifteen years with the Egyptian monks and then, setting up a monastery in the south of France, wrote his celebrated *Conferences* and *Institutes*, containing their teachings. His influence on St Benedict was very great.

By the time Benedict was born in Nursia (c. 480), monasticism had already existed for nearly two centuries. It was well established in the West as well as in the East, and all the Church Fathers of this period (except St Ambrose) at one time or another lived the monastic life. But in the West there was no generally accepted rule of life; the situation was chaotic, results very variable. The future reformer of this state of affairs, Benedict, studied at Rome, but as an adolescent betook himself to the hill country round Subiaco (fifty miles east of Rome) to live the life of a hermit in a cave there. However, as with Antony so with Benedict, disciples came. Eventually he found himself head of a large family, whom he organised in twelve small monasteries, retaining for himself the general supervision of them. About the year 530 he was persecuted by the local priest, and for the sake of peace emigrated with a few companions southwards. The site of his new monastery was on Monte Cassino, overlooking the highway from Rome to Naples. There, in the fullness of his experience, he wrote his Rule. This was to be a guide as to how men, living in community, should travel by a straight road to union of soul with God. He wrote for his own monks, but it is also clear from the text that he had other monasteries in mind, either in terms of reform or as new foundations. He writes with a mysterious authority as if he knew that his Rule would be widely accepted.

Pope Gregory the Great (590–604) wrote the life of Benedict, making use of the testimony of four old monks who had known him personally. What he has left us is mainly a collection of stories of a miraculous nature—the sort of thing that the scientific historian of the last century neither could nor would take seriously. However, if we allow for the kind of exaggerations or embellishments that take place when stories of the miraculous are repeated in community and passed on from one to another, it still remains that Benedict was remembered as this kind of person by those who had known him. There emerges a figure of great spiritual stature, whom God calls to serve him from his youth, and whom he rewards with outstanding gifts. Dom Justin McCann wrote:

It seems to me clear that his (St Gregory's) whole account is

> designed to portray St Benedict as endowed with that non-hierarchical charismatic authority which he ascribes also to the great Abbot Equitius (*Dialogues:* I, 4) and to others of his non-clerical monastic saints. It was definitely a period when conspicuous personal sanctity was considered to give spiritual authority. The laity accorded it . . . nor did the Bishops object.[1]

Charismatic in this sense means the quality of one who, while not called to any position in the Church's hierarchy, is yet led by the Holy Spirit along a distinctive spiritual path for the benefit of others. As they follow this path there comes to such men and women a spiritual authority arising from their pattern of holiness, which has a profound influence on others. Subsequent generations of their followers recognise in them 'the fullness of the Spirit'.

Gregory underlined also how rich Benedict was in the *charismata* of healing, prophecy and discernment. He noted, too, that Benedict's Rule would be a reflection of how he lived, and the Rule anticipates in those who follow it certain characteristics of a less startling kind which are nevertheless God-given gifts and signs of the effusion of the Spirit: the constant awareness of God's presence everywhere, the tears of compunction in prayer, the ready recognition of Christ in the man we meet or under whom we live, the prolongation of prayer under the influence of the Holy Spirit, the receiving of a 'Word' expressing God's will in a Community Chapter, a special gift of abstinence.

At Monte Cassino Benedict lived until his death, for which the date usually given is 547, and there he wrote his Rule. In it he did not repeat the system he had used

---

[1] *St Benedict*, p.116n. Sheed and Ward, 1937

at Subiaco of small monasteries gathered into one complex under his own supervision, but provided that all should live in the one monastery, divided if necessary, and as far as necessary, into groups of ten, under officials called deans.

He who sets out to create or regulate an alternative society undertakes a fairly comprehensive job, even if the society be on a small scale. He will have to consider motivation, i.e. for what purpose it exists or men should join it; it will need laws, and laws imply sanctions; it will have to treat of places and things; and of how to secure good relationships between its members. Above all he will have to be clear about what he is aiming at. All this Benedict contrived to set out in a remarkably short space, although we must always remember that he counts on a study of holy Scripture, particularly the Gospels, to supply a deeper understanding of his enactments. He counts, too, on the exposition of his thought by the Abbot in charge of the monastery. In his observances there is always a flexibility such that, while he creates a firm structure, he never loses sight of the possible need for adaptation to circumstances; there is always room for the Spirit to flow.

The modern reader, if he is interested in these matters at all, will probably feel sympathy with the intention to establish a way of life for fraternal communities. And if further dissatisfied with the barrenness of a materialistic society, however affluent, he finds himself in some way 'seeking God' (Ch. LVIII), he will be sympathetic also with the monastic orientation to prayer, which in fact relates to the monastic notion of a fraternal community, rather as the end relates to the means.

He may react less kindly to the heavy underlining of

the significance of humility. For Benedict it was sufficient argument to say, 'Scripture proclaims it loudly to us,' but in fact there are other grave reasons for teaching that humility is the necessary foundation which must be laid, if a man wishes to live closely with God. Experience had shown (and continuously shows) that spiritual achievements not based on humility could be dangerous illusions.

Likewise a modern reader may find the simple assumption of Ch. XLIX, that 'the life of a monk should be always lenten in spirit' unattractive. It is not that 'such strength is found only in the few' but that such an attitude is not accepted at all. The tendency to leave out the penitential aspects of the monastic life, and to regard them as belonging to a gloomy past, or to ignore them as irrelevant, is better faced than left to prevail unobserved or constitute a barrier to grasping the whole message. Benedict assumes that the monk accepts the need to do penance, and he is concerned only with deciding what is a reasonable measure. But what are the reasons for thinking it necessary at all? Christian tradition puts them thus:

1 We are sinners, and although Christ has atoned for our sins, it is right that we, too, should do penance for our sins. In fact, a willingness to do penance is a product of contrition, and there is no depth to a spiritual life that does not contain contrition.
2 The erection of a barrier against self-indulgence, which is the enemy of the life of the spirit.
3 An assimilation to Christ in the mystery of his self-denial, his death and resurrection. He who, rightly, desires to share in the joy of Christ's resurrection, must

also be willing to take up his Cross and follow him. Thus do we come to know him.

4 Akin to this, Christian tradition attributes to penance and to a penitential way of life an intercessory force; to enter into Christ's sufferings, is to receive a share of his power, and to be able to bring that power to the help and redemption of others.

Given this basis, there is still room for discussion on what forms of implementation best suit us today.

There are other aspects of the Rule, which a modern reader may find fearsome. We may table some of them thus:

Modern Tendency	*The Rule*
Dislike of authority	Presumption of strong authority
Small equipment in faith	Heavy demands on faith
Interested mainly in the *NOW*	Preoccupied with the Judgement
The Gospel is *only* Good News	The Gospel brings also warnings
Consume all you can!	Consumption based on need
Fulfil your personality!	Renounce your own will!
Escape from your inner emptiness	'Avoid forgetfulness'
Bustling, noisy, unrestrained	Insistence on silence
Contemptuous of the spirit world	Highly conscious of angels and devils

These antitheses are not necessarily irreconcilable, nor as total as they may seem; but it is true that a voice from another age is speaking to us, that it has different presuppositions, and is unaware of our slogans. Hence there is a need to examine carefully just what this voice is saying, neither avoiding what seems alien, nor interpreting it wrongly. Moreover, it is also possible to list a number of points in which the alternative society sketched out by the Rule seems markedly in accord with modern aspirations:

1 There is today a great current of search for the Transcendent. For such seekers Benedict undertook to provide a path; and he was a master who evidently speaks from experience.
2 The Rule abounds in practical directives concerning the way to form a close relationship with God,
3 and also in directives concerning human relationships.
4 The Rule is not written for individualists, but thinks in terms of fulfilment through community.
5 It sets up an ordered society, not governed by the pursuit of wealth.
6 It lays down equality in the social order.
7 It aims at stability of life—and is nevertheless flexible.
8 It is realistic; there is throughout a pervading sense of humanity. The spiritual life is not just a set of intellectual concepts but is related throughout to human conditions.
9 There is also an acceptance and recognition of the place of material things in one's philosophy of life, and, most notably,
10 a special feeling for the poor, the sick—indeed for anyone in need of protection.

The Rule is not a complete treatise of spirituality. Its aim is primarily to set up 'the household of God', and it contains: (i) legislation for that purpose; (ii) basic doctrine necessary for this kind of household; (iii) observances making up its daily life. These last derive their significance and value from being supports for the formation of true relationships with God and also with man, which is the object of the whole system. They are, therefore, subject to change according to time and place, as the author of the Rule was well aware. Moreover, as he explicitly states at the end, 'the Rule does not contain the observance of all justice.' It supposes a continuous study of Holy Scripture, and a growing understanding of their central doctrine—the Paschal Mystery. The monk is to learn to die and to live with Christ, to accept to share in his passion and to enjoy also the fruits of his resurrection. If we miss this—and it is alluded to, rather than explicitly propounded—we shall miss the deepest significance of this form of community life.

There are men, explained Don Quixote to Sancho Panza, who will turn a book loose on the world with as little dispatch as if it were a dish of fritters. A new translation of the Rule and a Commentary on it may call for justification.

The translation, indeed, is necessary, for otherwise the Commentary would be intelligible only to those well acquainted with the text. But why should the thoughts of Benedict of Nursia interest us today?

Undoubtedly there is, for a variety of reasons, widespread interest in community life, and not only among those who might be thinking of joining a religious order, but because of the general breakdown of community relationships in our modern world.

This little book is not intended for the learned brethren and sisters of the Order, whose libraries are well stocked with translations and commentaries, but is addressed to a wider public who may have an interest in spiritual classics in general and community living in particular. Hence archeology finds little place in the observations made; they are intended to make clear, and (in some places) relevant to today, the lines of Benedict's thought. They have been kept as brief as possible.

It may, however, be useful to explain here the background to the timetable set out in the Rule. The Romans, like ourselves, reckoned twenty-four hours to the day, and divided them into two sets of twelve. Unlike us they reckoned the day hours as corresponding to the period of light, and the night hours as corresponding to the period of darkness. Hence the length of each hour varied; in winter, when the darkness was longer, the hours of the night were each longer, and the hours during the day correspondingly shorter. Thus 'the eighth hour of the night' (Ch. VIII) would have been about 2 am at the equinox (22–3 Sept.), but later as the winter deepened. Hence it is not possible to give precise modern equivalents for each hour.

The headings of the chapters of the Rule are translations of the Latin; the headings of the chapters of the commentary are sometimes different; this is in order to indicate more clearly the contents of the chapter, which are in some cases more various than the Latin title suggests.

In doctrinal passages the Rule cites Scripture frequently, but not always in exact words; hence the translations given are intended to correspond to what is written and intended by the Rule, rather than to modern versions of Scripture. The references are therefore to the Vulgate.

The author wishes to thank particularly Dom Leo Williamson, OSB, MA, for help with the translation, Dom James Mitchell, OSB, PhL and Dom Laurence O'Keeffe, OSB, LLS, for reading the typescript and making helpful suggestions; and Miss Rosaleen O'Connor for her kindness in typing the manuscript; also Dom Cuthbert Smith, OSB, and Mrs Joan Street for proof-reading.

Finally, as the Order celebrates in 1980 a millennium and a half (480–1980) since the birth of St Benedict, this little work is intended also as a tribute to him, and it is written, to make use of words that embody his spirit, 'that God may be glorified in all things'.

Note

The traditional dates have been added in the margin for the benefit of any communities which may wish to use the text for reading aloud.

The Rule of Saint Benedict

Contents of the Rule of St Benedict

The Prologue

Listen my son to the instructions of your Master, turn Jan. 1 May 2
the ear of your heart to the advice of a loving father; Sept. 1
accept it willingly and carry it out vigorously; so that through the toil of obedience you may return to him from whom you have separated by the sloth of disobedience.[1] To you, then, whoever you may be, are my words addressed, who, by the renunciation of your own will, are taking up the strong and glorious weapons of obedience in order to do battle in the service of the Lord Christ, the true King.

First of all, whenever you begin any good work, you must ask of God with the most urgent prayer that it may be brought to completion by him, so that he who has now deigned to reckon us in the number of his sons, may not later on be made sad by our wicked actions. For we must at all times use the good gifts he has placed in us, so that he will not later on disinherit us as an angry father disinherits his sons; nor like a feared lord, who has been roused to anger by our sins, hand over to eternal punishment us wicked slaves for refusing to follow him to glory.

Let us then at last arouse ourselves, even as Scripture Jan. 2 May 3
incites us in the words, 'Now is the hour for us to rise Sept. 2
from sleep.'[2] Let us, then, open our eyes to the divine light, and hear with our ears the divine voice as it cries out to us daily. 'To-day if you hear his voice, do not harden your hearts,'[3] and again, 'He who has ears to

---

[1] cf. Bar 4:28 [2] Rom 13:11 [3] Ps 94:8

hear, let him hear what the Spirit says to the Churches.' [4] And what does the Spirit say? 'Come, my sons, listen to me; I shall teach you the fear of the Lord.' [5] 'Run while you have the light of life lest the darkness of death overwhelm you.'[6]

Jan. 3 May 4 Sept. 3 And as the Lord seeks his workman in the mass of people, he again cries out to him in the words, 'Who is the man who desires life and is eager to see Good Days?'[7] If you hear this and reply, 'I do,' God says to you, 'If you want to have true and everlasting life, keep your tongue from speaking evil, and your lips from uttering deceit. Turn aside from evil and do good; seek peace and follow after it.' [8] 'When you do this my eyes will be upon you, and my ears will be open to your prayers, and before you call upon me I shall say to you: "Here I am." ' [9] What can be sweeter to us than this voice of the Lord as he invites us, dearest brothers? See how, in his loving mercy, the Lord points out to us the Way of Life.[10]

Jan. 4 May 5 Sept. 4 Let us therefore make for ourselves a girdle out of faith and perseverance in good works, and under the guidance of the Gospel let us pursue our way in his paths, so that we may deserve to see him who has called us to his Kingdom. For if we wish to make our home in the dwelling-place of his Kingdom, there will be no getting there unless we run towards it by good deeds. But let us question the Lord with the prophet, saying to him, 'Lord, who shall make his home in your dwelling place; who shall rest on your holy mountain?' [11] And then let us listen to the Lord's answer to our question,

---

[4] Rev 2:7 [5] Ps 33:12 [6] cf. Jn 12:35 [7] Ps 33:12 [8] ibid. 13,14 [9] cf. Is 58:9
[10] cf. Ps 25:10; Acts 9:2; 19:9,23 [11] Ps 14:1

as he shows us the way to this dwelling-place, saying, 'He who walks without fault and does what is right; he who tells the truth in his heart; he who works no deceit with his tongue; he who does no wrong to his neighbour; he who does not slander his neighbour.' [12] 'He who casts the wicked devil, even as he beguiles him, out of the sight of his heart, along with the temptation itself, and so reduces him to impotence, and takes the incipient thoughts that he suggests and dashes them against (the rock of) Christ';[13] those who fear the Lord and do not become conceited about keeping the law well, but realise that the good in themselves cannot be their own work but is done by the Lord who is working in them, and so say with the prophet, 'Not unto us, Lord, not unto us, but unto your name, give the glory.'[14] For neither did the Apostle Paul give himself any credit for his preaching, but said, 'By the grace of God I am what I am.' [15] And the same Apostle also said, 'He who boasts must boast in the Lord.' [16]

And so the Lord also says in the Gospel, 'Everyone Jan. 5
who listens to these words of mine and acts on them, May 6 Sept. 5
will be like a sensible man who built his house on rock; floods rose, gales blew and hurled themselves against that house, and it did not fall; it was founded on rock.' [17] Thus the Lord concludes his reply, and daily expects us to respond through our dutiful actions to his holy precepts.

Therefore in order that amends may be made for sins, the days of our life are prolonged to give us a time in which to make our peace, as the Apostle says, 'Do you

---

[12] ibid. 2,3 [13] Ps 136:9 [14] Ps 113:1 [15] I Co 15:10 [16] 2 Co 10:17
[17] Mt 7:25

realise that the patience of God is meant to lead you to repentance?' [18] For this loving Lord says, 'I do not wish the death of the sinner, but that he should change his ways and live.' [19]

Jan. 6
May 7
Sept. 6
We have asked the Lord, my brothers, about the kind of man who dwells in his house, and we have heard what is required in order to do so. So let us fulfil the task of such a dweller. That means that we must make ready our hearts and bodies to engage in the warfare of holy obedience to his commands, and because our nature has not power to do this, we must ask God to send forth the help of his grace to our aid. And, if we wish to escape the punishment of hell and reach eternal life, then while there is still time, while we are still living in this body and this life gives us the light to do all these things, we must hurry to do now what will profit us for ever.

Jan. 7
May 8
Sept. 7
We propose, therefore, to establish a school of the Lord's service, and in setting it up we hope we shall lay down nothing that is harsh or hard to bear. But if for adequate reason, for the correction of faults or the preservation of charity, some degree of restraint is laid down, do not then and there be overcome with terror, and run away from the way of salvation, for its beginning must needs be difficult.[20] On the contrary, through the continual practice of monastic observance and the life of faith, our hearts are opened wide, and the way of God's commandments is run in a sweetness of love that is beyond words. Let us then never withdraw from discipleship to him, but persevering in his teaching in the monastery till death, let us share the sufferings of

---

[18] Rm 2:4 [19] Ezk 33:11 [20] Mt 7:14

Christ through patience, and so deserve also to share in his kingdom.

The Prologue

Listen my son

This style of introduction is borrowed from the Book of Proverbs[21] or that of Sirach[22]. We are present at an interview between an experienced religious teacher and one who has apparently reached a point in life when he realises that his life is not properly orientated. He belongs to a world that has been dislocated in its relationship with God the Creator. The real key to life is that God the Father has sent his Son to redeem the world, and the Son has redeemed it by fulfilling the command of his Father, and so by a wonderful act of obedience restored creation to its right relationship with God. The Saviour has done yet more, for by associating men to himself, through the adoption conferred in baptism, he makes them truly children of God. But these children of God do not always behave as they should; sometimes they behave much as if none of these things had happened, or as if they were mere beneficiaries without any positive role to play. They fail to realise that they are called on to serve him *with the good gifts he has placed in us* and, showing little interest in following the path to eternal glory, run the risk of being disinherited by God at the end.

The advice that follows is offered to anyone ('whoever-you-are') who has in mind to follow Christ, and realises, if rather vaguely, that as Christ wrought our salvation by his obedience to the Father[23] we should follow him by taking up the same *glorious weapons of obedience*. The word 'weapons' is not out of place, for Christ won a battle, indeed won the whole warfare against the powers of darkness, and the business of our life is to claim that victory for ourselves; we do this effectively by ranging ourselves behind the banner of Christ the true King.

To the person, then, in this condition, young or old, man or woman, comes an awareness that they are being invited 'to rise

---

[21] Pr 1:8; 2:1; 3:1 etc. [22] Sir 16:24 [23] Ph 2:7,8

from sleep', from the endless drifting of purposeless days, and that a divine call is making itself felt. *Today, if you hear his voice, do not harden your hearts*. Nor is this divine call to a more thorough-going service a matter exclusively for a few individuals, it is addressed to many: *He that has ears to hear let him hear what the Spirit says to the Churches*. Every human life has a vocation, for everyone is called in some way to fill a special place in God's Kingdom. The origin of a vocation is a call of the Spirit.

The teacher (*magister*) who puts forward these reminders is not the only teacher in Christ's Kingdom. But he knows from his life and experience a method of answering the call; and this he will expound to those interested. God does indeed call everybody, but not in the same way. And so a process of selection is shown at work. *The Lord seeks his workman among the mass of people*, and calls out: *Who is the man who desires life and is eager to see Good Days*? The metaphor is changed; where before whoever-you-are was thought of as a recruit about to join Christ's army, now he is invited to become a workman in God's workshop. Later a third metaphor will liken him to a pilgrim seeking his final home; and yet a fourth invitation, which is more than an image, will tell him that he is invited to become a disciple in the Lord's School.

I will teach you the fear of the Lord: We normally think of our fears, whether physical or psychological, as oppressive, corresponding to things to escape from. Nor does such fear need teaching; it is instinctive. What Scripture calls *fear of the Lord* is something quite different. It is the perception of our true relationship with our Almighty but All-loving Creator. And this is a blessing: *Happy the man who fears the Lord*.[24] It is the *beginning of wisdom*, the basis of true service of God. This perception, so far from being a defect or even an inferior quality (to be thrown out later), is one of the seven gifts of the Holy Spirit. As it is a basic necessity, it will be referred to constantly in the Rule, and be laid down as a requisite in every official. We must be very clear that while human fear crushes and diminishes our personality, this awareness of who God is and of his infinite power is the root of spiritual vitality; it is also the source of loving praise of him.

But what about these Good Days? What sort of reality is this? Does one think of joining a monastery in search of Good Days? In truth Good Days, in the deepest sense of the word, depend on two things: a full orientation towards our Creator, and the lively work-

---

[24] Ps 111:1

ings in us of the Holy Spirit, who alone brings to life in us the fruits of Christ's redemption.

There follows a warning: certain simple but indispensable dispositions are required in us, without which God cannot give the answer to our desires. *Keep your tongue from speaking evil*, turn away from whatever implies wrong-doing, be a man of true peace with all. These are the indispensable accompaniments of a sincere turning to God. With these reminders then, we are to be of good hope, for God says: *Ecce adsum, Look, I am here already*! . . . And at this thought the teacher seems to forget his context, and suddenly cries out: *What can be sweeter, dearest brothers, than this voice of the Lord, as he invites us*?

The next point to be made clear is that there is a journey ahead. Brother whoever-you-are is on a pilgrimage to his heavenly fatherland. The way is mapped out for him; if he follows the *guidance of the Gospel*, he will be on the right path. The Rule that follows will not offer him another path; it will merely 'declare' or set out the way to carry out the Gospel in the framework of a human society.

But it will be necessary on this journey to keep moving; otherwise *there will be no getting there at all*; and a good pace is recommended, since the sluggard will find the going all the heavier. But this running or good pace is not that of impatience or a kind of breathlessness about reaching journey's end; no, it is the performance of *good deeds* that sets the pace.

Having made this clear the teacher goes on to point out that since life is given in order that we may reach this terminus of our journey, it is in itself a limited space, in which we are to learn to fulfil the divine admonitions. We should not be caught before at any rate we have reached the milestone of true repentance for evil done, and God does not want to call us to him before that time. So *we must hurry to do now what will profit us for ever.*

The conclusion of these thoughts on the significance of human life is that it will be useful to set up a *School of the Lord's Service*, wherein those who enter will be taught how to prepare their hearts and bodies to obey the divine commands. The School will be a 'house of God', though the term is not used till later; that is to say it is conceived as a kind of local church or ecclesial unit, standing on its own ground, containing persons who have dedicated themselves anew to following the *way of God's Commandments*, a synonym for the Gospel; it has its own head, and is governed by its own laws, subject to the approval of the Church. It is there to provide the framework and the method of which Brother whoever-you-are stands in need to answer God's call.

Two further indications are given of what lies ahead. The new brother entering into this *way of life* must not be scared away if some restrictions are imposed on him; he will be sharing the lot of Christ who said, 'Unless a man renounce himself and take up his cross and follow me, he is not worthy of me.' [25] On the other hand he will discover that 'his heart will be opened wide (or enlarged) to make room for the unspeakable sweetness of God's love,' which he is destined to discover through his practice of monastic observance. For this is the deepest significance of the *Good Days* that are offered him: they are a sharing not only of the sufferings of Christ, but also in the goodness of his risen life.

---

[25] Mt 10:38

Preliminary Survey

Chapter I The Kinds of Monk

It is clear that there are four kinds of monk. Jan. 8 May 9 Sept. 8

The first kind are the Cenobites, that is the 'monastery' kind, who do battle under a Rule and an Abbot.

Then the second kind are the Anchorites or Hermits; these are they who are no longer in the first fervour of their religious life but have been tested for a long time in the monastery and have learnt, with the assistance of many brothers, how to do battle against the devil; and now, well equipped to leave the fraternal battle-line for the solitary combat of the desert, they are strong enough to do battle against the vices of the body or the mind on their own, with their own resources, relying on God's aid, but now without the support of anyone else.

The third kind of monk is the abominable one of Sarabaites, who have not been tested by a rule, as gold is tested in a furnace, nor been taught by experience, but are like soft lead. They keep faith with this world by their actions, but manifestly lie to God by their tonsure. These people live in twos and threes, or even alone; they have no shepherd, they shut themselves up in their own sheepfolds, not those of the Lord; and their law consists in yielding to their desires: what they like or choose they call holy, and they reckon illicit whatever displeases them. Jan. 9 May 10 Sept. 9

The fourth kind of monk are those called Wanderers. These are never stable throughout their whole lives but wanderers through diverse regions, receiving hospitality in the monastic cells of others for three or four days at a time, following their own wills, enslaved by the attractions of gluttony. They are in all respects worse than the Sarabaites.

It is better to pass over in silence than to speak further of the unhappy way of life of all these people, so let us pass them by, and with God's help set about organising the strongest kind of monks—the Cenobites.

The Kinds of Monk

The teacher takes a preliminary look round the world of monks of his day. He lists four kinds of *soi-disant* religious persons, and considers them in the light of their value as soldiers in Christ's army.

Hermits rank high, for they are regarded as already well trained and competent for their solitary battle.

'Sarabaites' on the other hand are weak to the point of uselessness, for their life in select little parties is lived without serious religious guidance; inevitably it will consist in pleasing themselves.

They keep faith with this world . . . lie to God by their tonsure: The modern monk is not recognisable by his tonsure; he neither lies to God nor asserts anything by his hair-style. But the need to break visibly with the ways of this world, and to assert something very definitely by one's life-style becomes more and more urgent as our society plunges morally into the abyss, and socially into disruption. The need is for witnesses whose witness is both intelligible and unmistakable, for witnesses who know how to reject and rebuke evil however disguised, and likewise proclaim what is good.

The 'Wanderers' represent the collapse of an ideal that demanded too much of human nature altogether. For they set out to be, not so much poor, as destitute of home or means of subsistance, and end up by being scroungers for a night's lodging or a meal wherever they can. They produce no spiritual fruit at all.

To be practical then, says St Benedict, one must have a monastery (*Coenobium*) in which the monk has *the assistance of many brothers*. These are the elements that make for strength in the monastic state.

But what exactly is a Rule? It will no doubt contain the insights of the teacher, gained from a long experience of guiding souls, but in essence it is a framework organising a community so that it may carry out the Gospel in all its implications. Inevitably such a document will draw on the Acts of the Apostles, from which we learn most of what we know about the first Christian community.[1]

There are, however, great differences between the monastic group and the first Christian community, for the former limits itself to a number of persons who make a free commitment to a complete pattern of life; moreover, the sexes draw apart. And the groupings are charismatic, i.e. based on the response of the individual to the call of the Spirit, and on personal experience, rather than hierarchic in structure. The Rule was a necessary guide.

Moreover, such a group, not being based on a hierarchical or sacramental principle, had to find a leader in its own way and of its own kind. Hence he is mentioned here as an essential element in the cenobitic life.

The monastery, the Rule, the Abbot; with the mention of these three the nature of the School of divine service or the house of God has been indicated.

---

[1] Ac 2:42–7; 4:32–7; 5:1–11

1
The Formation and Nature of the Monastery

Chapter II What Kind of Man the Abbot should be

An Abbot who is worthy to be in charge of a monastery must always bear in mind what he is called and fulfil in his actions the name of one who is called greater.[1] For he is believed to act in the place of Christ in the monastery, since he is called by his title, as the Apostle says, 'You have received the Spirit of adoption as sons, through whom we cry, Abba! Father!'[2] Therefore the Abbot should not teach or ordain or command anything that lies outside the Lord's commands, far from it; but his commands and his teaching should mingle like the leaven of divine justice in the minds of his disciples. The Abbot must always remember that at the fearful judgement of God two things will be discussed: his own teaching and the obedience of his disciples. The Abbot must also realise that whatever lack of fruitfulness the Father of the family may find in his sheep will be blamed on the shepherd. And likewise if the shepherd has laboured with complete diligence over a troublesome and disobedient flock, and has expended every care over their diseased behaviour, he will be acquitted in the Lord's judgement and will say with the prophet, 'I have not hidden your justice in my heart, but I have spoken of your truth and saving help';[3] 'but they have contemptuously despised me.'[4] And then finally the penalty of death will swallow up the sheep who were disobedient to his care.

Jan. 10
May 11
Sept. 10

---

[1] Mt 18:4 [2] Rm 8:15 [3] Ps 39:11 [4] Is 1:2

Jan. 11 May 12 Sept. 11 When, therefore, anyone takes the name of Abbot, he should rule over his disciples with two kinds of teaching; that is to say, he must show forth all good and holy things by his words and even more by his deeds. To apt disciples he must explain the Lord's teaching by word, but to those who are hard of heart or simple of mind he must make clear the divine teaching by his actions. By his deeds he must make it clear that nothing may be done which he has taught his disciples to be forbidden, lest while he preaches to others he should merit rejection himself, and God should some day say to him as he sins, 'What business have you reciting my statutes, standing there mouthing my covenant, since you detest my discipline, and thrust my words behind you?' [5] And 'you observed the splinter in your brother's eye, and did not notice the plank in your own?' [6]

Jan. 12 May 13 Sept. 12 The Abbot must not show personal preferences in his monastery. He must not be more loving to one than to another, unless he has found him to be more advanced in good works or in obedience. A free-born man must not be preferred to one entering the monastery from slavery, unless some other reasonable cause exists. But if it seems to the Abbot that there is good reason for it, let him do so, and let him do the same about the rank of any one. Otherwise let them keep their normal order. For whether we are slaves or freemen, we are all one in Christ, and serve on equal terms in the army of one Lord; 'for God has no favourites.' [7] In regard to rank we find distinction in his eyes only if we are found humble and better than others in good works. Therefore the Abbot should show himself equally loving to

[5] Ps 49:16,17 [6] Mt 7:3 [7] Rm 2:11

all, and maintain discipline impartially according to the merits of each.

In his teaching the Abbot should always observe the method of the Apostle, 'Employ arguments, appeals and rebukes.'[8] He must behave differently at different times, sometimes using threats, sometimes encouragement. He must show the tough attitude of a master, and also the loving affection of a father. Thus he should sternly reprimand the undisciplined and unruly, but entreat the obedient, the meek and the patient to go forward in virtue; as for the careless and the scornful, we instruct him to rebuke and correct them. He should not pretend that he does not see the faults of offenders, but remember the danger overhanging Eli, priest of Shiloh and, as best he can, he should cut them out by the roots as soon as they begin to show themselves. He should correct upright and intelligent minds with verbal admonitions once or twice, but the shameless, the thick-skinned and the proud or disobedient, he should repress at the very beginning of their sinful ways with the corporal punishment of blows, bearing in mind what is written, 'The fool is not corrected by words,'[9] and again, 'Strike your son with the rod and you will deliver his soul from death.'[10] Jan. 13 May 14 Sept. 13

The Abbot should always bear in mind what he is; he should bear in mind what he is called; and let him realise that more is demanded of him to whom more is entrusted. He must realise also how difficult and arduous is the task he has undertaken, that of ruling souls and serving men of many different characters: one, indeed, to be encouraged, another to be rebuked, Jan. 14 May 15 Sept. 14

[8] 2 Tm 4:2 [9] cf. Pr 19:29 [10] cf. Pr 19:18; 23:14

another persuaded, each according to his nature and intelligence. Thus he must adapt and fit himself to all, so that not only will he not lose any of the flock entrusted to him, but he will rejoice as his good flock increases.

Jan. 15 May 16 Sept. 15 It is most important that he should not pay greater attention to transient earthly things that pass away, and so fail to recognise or underestimate the salvation of the souls entrusted to him. Let him always consider that it is souls that he has undertaken to rule, and for whom he will give an account. Moreover, in order that he may not complain of reduced temporal goods, let him remember the Scripture, 'seek his Kingdom first, and his righteousness, and all these other things will be given you as well,' [11] and again, 'Nothing is lacking to those who fear him.' [12] Let him realise that he who undertakes to rule souls must prepare himself to give an account, whatever the number of brethren under his care. He must understand clearly that he will have to render an account on the Day of Judgement for all these souls, in addition, of course, to his own. Thus as he bears ever in mind the enquiry that will be made on the shepherd's care of the sheep entrusted to him, the thought that he takes concerning the accounts to be rendered for others, will make him careful of his own state. And so, while he provides by his instructions for the amendment of others, he will be brought also to the amendment of his own faults.

The Office of the Abbot

1 The first steps in the construction of the house of God are to set

[11] Mt 7:33 [12] Ps 33:10

in position the human stones of which it is made. In a certain sense the Abbot is the foundation stone, and he has a key role in the building. The essence of it is contained in the words: *He is believed to act in the place of Christ* in the community. That is the kind of leader he is called on to be. 'The role of the Abbot is in the realm of the charismatic, that of the Bishop ontologically sacramental.' [13] His role is that of fathership. This 'service gift' comes to him when he is made Abbot (*see* LXIV), and his position depends on this belief, as the Rule explains, quoting the text: *You have the Spirit of adoption as sons, whereby we cry 'Abba, Father'.* The text fits a bit clumsily here, but is intended to convey that the relationship is a spiritual one, and based on our capacity as adopted sons of God to choose one of ourselves as an instrument for receiving God's paternal guidance. This is the central theme; it has nothing to do with the lawyer's concept of jurisdiction.

2 No doubt the acceptability of such a doctrine is hindered in our civilisation by our decreased sense of the value and dignity of fatherhood. Democrats in our social and political life, we tend to transfer the same processes of thought to the religious sphere. Moreover, the human background in which we form our first notions of paternity too often gives us a sadly inadequate or even false concept of it. We associate it with authority, power, authoritarianism, prohibition, contestation, even out-of-date opinions. We fail to think in terms of care, love, protection, gentleness, guidance, providence, understanding. Very often a failure to understand paternity at the human level impedes us in our relationship with God our Father. We respond to him in the uncomfortable, distrustful terms, which are the only ones we know. An understanding of the role of paternity in the religious life is then something to be recovered, not thrown away. The doctrine set out in this chapter is indeed alien to much current thinking; nevertheless the setting up of the house of God on the model of a human family in which the spiritual functions of the father are brought to fulfilment contains a deep insight into our human needs. Clearly there is a need to understand the relationship spiritually, and not as the prolongation of a state of immaturity in the disciple.

3 We must recognise, too, that especially in our times effort may be necessary to bridge the credibility gap, so that the fruits of grace

---

[13] Emmanuel Lanne

intended to flow through the exercise of spiritual paternity may do so. The Rule foresees that such a gap would be insurmountable if the Abbot were unworthy of his role or failed to understand it. Here at some length and constantly throughout the Rule he is reminded of the all-searching judgements of God, and of the qualities he must cultivate. Primarily his job concerns the spiritual welfare of the community and of each member of it.

4 What of his administrative burdens? These can be heavy, even when shared by others. It can happen, too, that heavy burdens come, not from the duties laid down in the Rule, but from an inherited situation, which imposes upon the Abbot whole sets of duties and social or ecclesiastical obligations of which the Rule knows nothing. We recognise this situation very clearly when it is seen in the Middle Ages or Baroque times, but often enough it is no less a factor in our own. As long as these factors fit with the spirit of the Church of the times and are accepted by the brethren as such, all may be well, but when the ecclesial attitude and general atmosphere change there arises a difficult situation, since history does not willingly go into reverse. Simplification may become urgent and yet be an arduous and daunting business.

5 The correction of faults, on which the Rule insists, is not an easy part of the Abbot's task. In fact, unless it is based on a positive relationship of mutually cultivated confidence and trust and encouragement, it will prove impossible. Normally a community expects an Abbot to correct faults, since in practice we all suffer from one another's faults; with this expectation should go adequate moral support and understanding when he sets about it. A lack of this would indicate an inadequate sense of social responsibility. The correction of faults, however, is only the negative side of a process, of which the positive side is encouragement in the development of virtue. And the positive side is the more important. Moreover, unless the brethren are able to give trust and love and to receive it, the whole process will prove tiresome indeed, and the Abbot's specific charisma or service gift will be reduced to the task of keeping a good show of order and discipline. The Rule insists a good deal on this aspect of the Abbot's task. It is likely to show less visible return than some others, e.g., a building programme or an external apostolate. Hence, the depth and reality of the Abbot's faith in his central mission, and his self-sacrificing love, are bound to be tested.

6 The Abbot is to treat all, whether highly born or humbly born, with equal love and care. It is very easy for somebody to feel less loved or less cared for; some indeed have a predisposition that way, and this makes a problem. It is one of the great strides forward of our day that (after centuries of the opposite) social equality has been restored between all the members of God's household. But in the end the law cannot achieve true equality, and it is a matter of personal application to be borne constantly in mind. Here, surely, is a message for the monks to pass on to an embittered world.

7 The fact that a man has lacked a true relationship with his father and still feels the need of one does not make him a natural candidate for a monastery. This would be an illusion. Nor on the other hand is he automatically disqualified. The healing of a psychological wound and the finding of a religious vocation are not to be confused as one process.

8 Young religious, who expect their superior to be alert to what the Spirit is doing in them, are not in error, but they should also recognise what the Spirit may have to say to them through their superior. And for this reason we all need to pray for our superiors that they may be channels of God's guidance to us.

Chapter III On summoning the Brethren to Council

Jan. 16 May 17 Sept. 16 Whenever anything important has to be done in the monastery the Abbot must assemble the whole community and explain what is under consideration. When he has heard the counsel of the brethren, he should give it consideration and then take what seems to him the best course. The reason why we say that all should be called to council is this: It is often to a younger brother that the Lord reveals the best course. But the brethren must give their counsel submissively and humbly and not presume stubbornly to defend their opinions. The decision should, however, depend mainly on the Abbot's judgement, and all should be joined in obedience to what he considers the soundest course. But just as it is fitting that disciples should obey their master, so it is incumbent on him to settle everything with foresight and justice.

Jan. 17 May 18 Sept. 17 In every circumstance, therefore, all should follow the authority of the Rule, nor is it to be rashly abandoned by anyone. No one in the monastery is to follow the prompting of his own heart; no one is to presume to argue rudely with the Abbot, or to argue at all outside the monastery. If anyone does so presume, he must submit to disciplinary measures. The Abbot himself, however, in all his actions must fear God and keep the Rule, bearing in mind that most surely he will have to render account for all his decisions before God, the most just judge.

If, however, there are less important matters to be transacted for the well-being of the monastery, the

Abbot should take counsel only with the senior monks, for it is written, 'Take counsel about all you do and afterwards you will have no regrets.' [1]

The Community in Council

1 The community are the living stones of which the house of God is built. In this chapter they are shown exercising their responsibility as the Christian family, advising its father on a serious matter of significance to all. The meeting is not a parliament nor a debating society. It is God's family whose business it is to seek what may be the divine will in the matter in hand. All should be present, the skilful, the eloquent, the learned if there are any, but also the ordinary folk, the average, the young. All may offer their view to the Abbot whose business it is to discern the will of God. Prophecy, or at least the clear utterance of God's message, is not ruled out. God may use a younger person for this purpose; this is not because the young are wiser than their seniors; but God may more easily declare some new thing through one as yet free from the fixity that besets later years. He may be more open to the Spirit of God.

Nor in these deliberations should the guidance of the Rule be forgotten.

2 Was the procedure too idealistic to remain the norm indefinitely? Certainly the Canon Law of the Church has long decided that in a large number of matters the community's will shall prevail, at least negatively. To-day the Abbot cannot in many matters proceed without the community's consent; neither can the community compel the Abbot to take steps contrary to his judgement. Likewise the occasions when the Abbot has to take counsel with the seniors have been organised and clarified by Canon Law.

3 In the sixth century the world was politically and socially violent; but the harm that man could do to the natural world that supported him was limited. Armies might lay waste the land and produce starvation; but the land would recover; devastated buildings could be rebuilt. Nowadays the problems that a monastery may find

---

[1] Sir 32:19

itself involved in are much greater than then: they may be ecological, social, technological . . . Monks can hardly be expected to know all the answers, but they are witnesses to the Gospel; as such they have an involvement in the welfare of God's creation, and a responsibility for their attitude to it. This means that the decisions taken by a monastery today may well have to be weighed in terms of the larger issues of the good and evil tendencies of our times. They are going to need great purity of heart.

Chapter IV The Tools of Good Works

1 In the first place to love the Lord God with all one's heart, with all one's soul and with all one's strength[1] Jan. 18 May 19 Sept. 18

2 Then to love one's neighbour as oneself[2]

3 Then not to kill

4 Not to commit adultery

5 Not to steal

6 Not to covet

7 Not to bear false witness

8 To honour all men[3]

9 Not to do to another what one would not wish to have done to oneself

10 To deny oneself in order to follow Christ

11 To punish one's body

12 Not to seek pleasures

13 To love fasting

14 To relieve the poor

15 To clothe the naked

16 To visit the sick

17 To bury the dead

18 To give help in trouble

19 To console the sorrowful

20 To avoid worldly behaviour

21 To set nothing before the love of Christ

22 Not to give way to anger Jan. 19 May 20 Sept. 19

23 Not to cherish an opportunity for displaying one's anger

24 Not to preserve deceit in one's heart

---

[1] Mt 22:37 [2] ibid. 39 [3] I P 2:17

25 Not to give the kiss of peace insincerely
26 Not to abandon charity
27 Not to swear, for fear of perjury
28 To speak with one's mouth the truth that lies in one's heart
29 Not to return evil for evil
30 Not to inflict any injury, but to suffer injuries patiently
31 To love one's enemies[4]
32 Not to curse anyone who curses us, but instead to return a blessing
33 To suffer persecution for righteousness' sake
34 Not to be arrogant
35 Not given to drinking
36 Not a heavy eater
37 Not given to much sleeping
38 Not lazy
39 Not a grumbler
40 Not a detractor
41 To rest one's hope in God
42 Whenever one perceives any good in oneself to attribute it to God, not to one's self
43 But to recognise that whatever is evil is one's own doing, and to blame one's self

Jan. 20
May 21
Sept. 20

44 To fear the Day of Judgement [5]
45 To dread hell
46 To yearn for eternal life with all possible spiritual desire
47 To keep death daily before one's eyes
48 At every moment to keep watch over the actions of one's life

---

[4] Mt 5:43 [5] Mt 10:28

49 In every place to know that God most surely beholds one

50 To dash the evil thoughts that invade one's heart immediately upon Christ, as upon a rock, and to reveal them to one's spiritual father

51 To guard one's mouth against evil and vicious speech

52 Not to love much talking

53 Not to utter words that are foolish and provoke laughter

54 Not to love much or unrestrained laughter

55 To listen willingly to devout reading

56 To fall often to prayer

57 In our daily prayer to God to confess with tears and groans the wrong-doing in our past life

58 To amend these wrong ways in the future

59 To reject carnal desires

60 To hate one's own will

61 To obey the Abbot's commands in everything, even though he himself, (which God forbid) acts otherwise, remembering always that command of the Lord's, 'Do what they tell you, but do not do the things that they do' [6]

62 To be unwilling to be called holy before one is so, but to be holy first so that it may be more truly said of one

63 To carry out God's commands daily in one's actions Jan. 21 May 22 Sept. 21

64 To love chastity

65 To hate no one

66 Not to cherish bitterness

67 Not to indulge in envy

---

[6] Mt 23:3

68 Not to love quarrelling
69 To flee vainglory
70 To revere the elders
71 To love the young
72 To pray for one's enemies in the love of Christ
73 After a quarrel to make peace with the other before sunset
74 And never to despair of God's mercy

These then are the tools of the spiritual craft. If we make full use of them unceasingly day and night, then, when we give them back on the Day of Judgement, we shall in return receive from the Lord that reward which he himself has promised, 'The things that no eye has seen, and no ear has heard, which God has prepared for those who love him.' [7] Now the workshop in which we make diligent use of all these tools is the enclosure of the monastery combined with stability in the community.

The Tools of Good Works

This compilation of spiritual maxims follows in the tradition of the Desert Fathers. They made use of such collections of short sayings which formed the 'elements of a directory of the monastic life' for the use of beginners. The object was not to inculcate observances, but to teach discernment. This chapter could almost be entitled 'Aids to Discernment', i.e. to that quality which enables a man to distinguish between good and evil in the circumstances of his life, to recognise temptations, to understand what will prove helpful to him, to avoid illusions. Except for the beginning and the end, the order of the tools is not important, but there are obvious groupings.

In the first place to love the Lord . . . then one's neighbour (1,2):[8]

---

[7] I Co 2:9 [8] The numbers refer to Ch. IV of the Rule

Thus our Lord [9] traced out the whole horizon of man's earthly duties. These two precepts are put in the first place to indicate that all else is but a filling in of the consequences of these two principles. They cover our true relationship with God and our true relationship with man. The Rule itself is primarily about these two relationships, providing subordinate clauses on how to fulfil them; observances have meaning only in this context. Thoughts, words and actions will be judged good or evil by their contribution to the fulfilment of these two laws or their hindrance to such fulfilment.

If there is a third relationship to be considered, viz. one's attitude to oneself, it is to be found a little lower down in the list: *to deny oneself to follow Christ* (10). This also is a basic element in Christ's teaching.[10] The denial called for is not that of the Stoic, but of the Christian whose self-denial means a dying to sin, with Christ, in order that he may be able to share in the risen life of his Master. This will be carried out through entering into the Paschal mystery.

It is unwise to dismiss as conquered, temptations which have not yet fully declared themselves. There are gross temptations (3–7) which may suddenly steal up on a man, knock him out at a single blow and dislocate his whole life.[11] Scripture shows us how, in the life of King David, a wandering glance lets loose the sequence—adultery, lies, treachery, murder and near ruin. There are also simple precepts in which a man may fail because he does not examine his response to them carefully (8,9). Do we really *honour all men*?

If gross temptations can come suddenly upon a man, not because he is bad but because he is incautious, there are gross habits into which he may step gradually, unaware of the kind of person he is becoming. The gift of discernment keeps us on guard lest we become that very caricature of a monk who has always been the sport of his enemies (34–40).

But more especially do we need discernment in subtler temptations. For example:

Not to preserve deceit in one's heart (24)

When one perceives any good in oneself to attribute it to God, not to one's self (42)

And then we must learn to deal with evil thoughts promptly and courageously by confession of them (50). The point is: discern first, then take strong action.

Another group deals with the recognition of temptations that

---

[9] Mt 22:37–40 [10] Mt 8:34; 16:24; Lk 9:33 [11] cf. II S 11:2–17

test purity of heart. Not only concupiscence but anger is an impurity with manifold effects: whether it be a sudden upsurge, the slow fire of a grudge, the ill-will concealed in a cloak of politeness, the external granting of peace where is no forgiveness (22–28). The object of this set of maxims is to pinpoint the ways by which human perversity can abandon charity, or get round paying the true cost. It is followed by another short group (29–33) in which our Lord's standards of true love are recalled.

To hate one's own will (60) can be a dangerous maxim in the hands of the unskilled. It is based on the assumption that we are self-centred, and sin-prone, and it is this disorientated disposition which 'our own will' inevitably sets out to translate into practice. This is a will in the wrong direction. Our business is to unite our will constantly with God's, so that our will identifies itself with his. Psychologically speaking it is still our will, very much so, but reorientated and operating in God's way.

The positive values to be acquired will proceed from the resolution: *To set nothing before the love of Christ* (21). For it is not the routine of monastic life that sanctifies; no routine will ever sanctify. It is the act of the human will at each little crossroads, as it occurs in the individual life, saying yes to that choice which identifies with the Saviour's good pleasure, that means progress. So we assent to God's will to make us holy, even as his Son made himself holy for us.[12]

Love of God and one's neighbour will be but a sickly plant unless it nourishes itself in positive actions of Christian charity, and this especially towards those in need. A short list of maxims, mainly it would seem of persons outside the monastery, reminds us of this reality (14–19). We deceive ourselves unless we recognise Christ in human sufferers; it is a point of discernment. Nor are one's brethren to be forgotten (70–1).

Moreover, it is unprofitable to lead a life based on ascetic teachings unless there is an appreciation and love of what we pledge ourselves to.

Hence the form of the maxims:

To love fasting (13)
To love chastity (64)
implies a discernment of spiritual good perceived in what could otherwise be negative practices. Likewise *to listen willingly to devout reading* (55) implies a mind anxious to acquire spiritual values.

---

[12] Jn 17:19

Then there are maxims centring round the theme of recollection and what to be recollected about. For prayer is of the essence of the quest for God (56–7) and prayer is enshrined in recollection (44–9) which in its turn has an ally in silence (51–4).

And finally, whether things go ill or well, our true grounds of confidence lie in God's mercy (74).

At the end of the chapter the use of the tools is explained. They are the thoughts and actions with which to fill our days in God's service. For the most part they cannot be imposed by the Rule for they concern interior understanding. Throughout the Rule there is frequent insistence on the doctrine that it is by their interior quality—willingness or unwillingness, humility or pride, loving zeal or spirit of competition—that actions are to be judged. On the Day of Judgement only will the workman's task be over, and there will be no further need of these tools. The tool-box can be handed over to God. Till then, for the monk, the normal place to employ them is the monastery.

The household of God will be marked by certain characteristic virtues. It is also a school of divine service and the three virtues singled out for special attention in the next chapters—Obedience, Silence, Humility—are all the virtues of the learner. They are none of them distinguished for their popularity in human society as a whole. But it is clear that they are basic to the kind of society the Rule sets out to create.

Chapter V Obedience

Jan. 22
May 23
Sept. 22

The first step in humility is prompt obedience. This is fitting for those who hold nothing more dear to them than Christ, whether because they have made profession of holy service or for fear of hell or to attain the glory of everlasting life. Immediately when something has been commanded by a superior, it is for them as a divine command which knows no delay in its execution. The Lord says of them, 'As soon as he heard me, he obeyed me.'[1] And he said also to those who are to teach, 'Whoever listens to you listens to me.'[2]

Such men, therefore, at once leave whatever they are engaged on, abandon their own will, and with hands set free by leaving unfinished what they were doing, with the quick feet of obedience, follow by action the voice of him who gives the order. And so it is as if in a single moment the order of the master is uttered and the work of the disciple is completed with the speed inspired by the fear of the Lord. The two things are swiftly completed together by those in whose hearts lies the desire of reaching eternal life. Thus they take the narrow way, as the Lord says, 'Narrow is the way that leads to life.'[3] So they do not live according to their own wills, nor obey their own desires and pleasures, but behaving in accordance with the rule and judgement of another, they live in monasteries and desire to have an Abbot ruling over them. Without doubt such men imitate the mind of the Lord in his saying, 'I came to do not my own will, but that of him who sent me.'[4]

---

[1] Ps 17:44 [2] Lk 10:16 [3] Mt 7:14 [4] Jn 6:38

This obedience of which we speak will be acceptable to God and agreeable to men if what is ordered is carried out without fearfulness, without slowness in performance, without half-heartedness or grumbling or an unwilling reply. For the obedience that is shown to superiors is shown to God; for he said himself, 'He who listens to you, listens to me.'[5] And it should be offered by the disciples with good will, because 'God loves a cheerful giver.'[6] For if a disciple obeys grudgingly, if he complains not only in words but even in thought, then, although he carries out the order it will not now be acceptable to God, who sees that his heart is grumbling; and for work like this he will get no reward—indeed, he incurs the penalty for grumblers, unless he make amends with penance. Jan. 23 May 24 Sept. 23

Obedience

1 The theme most stressed in the 'Rule for beginners' is humility; and its first exterior manifestation will be a willingness to obey. The motives supplied for obedience in this chapter may seem a bit trite, but the essence of the matter lies in the sentence, *This obedience suits* (or *is fitting for*) *those who hold nothing more dear to them than Christ.* For God the Son became man in the spirit of obedience, as he himself tells us; this obedience was carried out sweetly during the long years of his home life with Mary and Joseph, and then carried to the limit of human sacrifice when he showed himself obedient unto death, even unto the death of the Cross.[7] The business of a Christian is then to imitate him in this essential characteristic of his life—his obedience to the Father, carried out through the submission shown to creatures. This will be done through the seeing of Christ specifically in one whom the community has elected as superior, of whom it is believed that he has the role of

---

[5] Lk 10:16 [6] II Co 9:7 [7] Ph 2:8

representing Christ as he taught and guided his band of Apostles. Commands then are to be obeyed, as divine commands would be, and this plays a significant part in producing the man ever prompt and ready to fulfil his Master's will with his whole heart.

2 This method has other values. For the spiritual beginner is liable to fall into various errors; a very common one is to suppose that God's will is to produce that improved version of himself, which is what he takes for holiness. Whereas God's will is essentially the production of 'a new creature', of divine conceiving, endowed with new possibilities of mind and heart, rich in God-given qualities. Obedience then will help one travelling along this path to avoid errors and self-deceit; and most importantly it will free him from attachment to his own will. It is not that he will cease to have a will, but that being set free, his will becomes identified with that of God. And the Rule, always concrete, teaches the beginner that the act of obedience, to do its work, has to be wholehearted, otherwise it will not produce its fruits.

3 Is there not much to be said by way of objection to, rejection of, or limitation of obedience? Is not a permanent state of obedience a menace to the growth of personality? What about human rights? What if the superior gets it wrong etc.?

The Rule seems aware only of the last of these objections. For this reason it constantly reminds the Abbot to bear in mind God's judgements at every moment, even as he makes his own decisions. To-day such decisions inevitably take in a wider span of considerations, having regard to intellectual and psychological needs and future activities. More than ever before does the Abbot need to aim at identification of his own acts of will with those of the divine Master, for his rights to be obeyed as a master and listened to as a teacher stem from this willingly conceded position that he acts on behalf of Christ. The essential aim of obedience—the production of the new man in Christ—remains unchanged, but the equipment required by this new man in today's Church is much altered.

4 And if it goes wrong? If the superior one way or another produces wrong judgements or fails to show sufficient love? What then? Certainly there will be suffering and loss; but the monk in such a situation will bear in mind that it is ultimately to Christ that he vowed obedience, ultimately Christ who accepted his trust, and that Christ will not fail him. Indeed when his faith and trust undergo most tension then surely is he most near to Christ, provided that he stands firmly in his trust. Must he give more than he realised before? Christ will offer more too. There is no suffering that Christ will not repay beyond conceiving. He is that kind of Master.

5 And what of other objections? If reaching maturity was not a preoccupation in St Benedict's day, it certainly is in our own. There is, however, a difference between spiritual and psychological maturity. The attainment of the latter is not properly the object of the Rule, which takes for granted that it will be reached. However, where psychological immaturity is found it calls for its own appropriate handling—something, in its technical aspects, outside the teachings of the Rule. The reaching of spiritual maturity is very much the object of the Rule's teaching: Chapters IV–VII are much concerned with it.

What of human rights? Certainly anyone who is preoccupied with the assertion of his own human rights should not join a monastery. If Christ had been preoccupied with his rights there would have been no crucifixion, and no redemption. But he 'emptied himself' for the sake of us who are sinners. The question is whether we who are sinners will take the risk of emptying ourselves, i.e. depriving ourselves of what we are entitled to, in return? The choice has to be free, enlightened, and deliberate. But that there is a division of the ways should not be denied; and therefore all relevant considerations should be weighed.

6 Grumbling: see Chapters XL, Section 3, and XLI.

Chapter VI On keeping silent

Jan. 24 May 25 Sept. 24 Let us do what the prophet says, 'I have resolved: I will watch how I behave and not let my tongue lead me into sin; I set a muzzle over my mouth; I stayed dumb, I was humbled, I refrained from speaking even good words.' [1] Here the prophet teaches that if we should sometimes for the sake of the virtue of silence refrain even from good conversation, we should all the more, for fear of the penalty of sin, refrain from evil words. Therefore, because of the great importance of keeping silence, permission to speak should be rarely given even to exemplary disciples, for conversation that is good and holy and edifying; for it is written, 'If you talk a lot you will not escape falling into sin,' [2] and elsewhere, 'Death and life are in the power of the tongue.' [3] Indeed it is fitting for the master to talk and to teach; the disciple's part is to keep silent and to listen.

Therefore, if it is necessary to ask a superior for something, the request should be made with humility and submissive reverence. But as for loose talk, idle words and talk that stimulates laughter, we condemn this with a permanent ban in all places, and we do not allow a disciple to open his mouth in this kind of speech.

Restraint in Speech

If obedience is not the world's most popular virtue, neither is silence a winner. This chapter does not concern rules for silence, but is about a virtue referred to in Latin as *taciturnitas*. This meant a love

---

[1] Ps 38:2,3 [2] Pr 10:19 [3] Pr 18:21

of keeping silent, reticence, the having mastered the tendency to gossip or babble, the having acquired a curb of one's tongue. But what makes that a virtue?

We may note that while the theme is not raised in the Gospels, yet attention to it is paid elsewhere in Scripture. It was seen as having the authority of Holy Writ. Why was it thought important?

1 This silence and absence of even harmless babble permits of the hearing of the Lord's voice at other times of the day than prayer. And this is a reality to be awaited, hoped for and recognised when it comes. There may be periods in a monk's life when the Lord does not appear to be communicative, does not make his presence felt, but not for that reason should 'Israel's watch on the Lord' be abandoned. The injunction 'Watch and pray' is a very real one for a charismatic community, and the watch extends outside the times of fixed prayer. There is about this silence a deliberate virginal emptiness, a readiness to receive the Word of God, such as was in Mary when she conceived the Word. The first significance of silence is to permit recollection which in its turn permits of the reception of the divine message.

2 The doctrine of silence is of value not only for those who lead an enclosed life. Let us hear Mother Teresa of Calcutta:

> We need to find God, and he cannot be found in noise and restlessness. God is the friend of silence. See how nature—trees, flowers, grass—grows in silence. The more we receive in prayer the more we can give in the active life. We need silence to be able to touch souls. The essential thing is not what we say but what God says through us.[4]

3 A reason for practising this virtue heavily underlined in the Rule is that so often we do harm with our tongues. Given a heart that is impure, what is likely to come out of our mouth? If we keep down our natural tendency to gossip, the first casualties of our restraint will be such things as detraction, vainglory, grumbling etc., with corresponding gain to ourselves and to those who would otherwise have heard us.

4 There are more problems concerning the practice of silence than can be discussed here, viz. the effects of certain forms of work on

---

[4] Quoted from *Something Beautiful for God*, Malcolm Muggeridge, Collins, 1971

the way of life of a monastery, the need we experience for recreational periods, the admission of the media of communication into the cloister. Clearly the media of communication are not bad in themselves, may be valuable, are capable of performing useful service to God's Kingdom. On the other hand we must recognise that while they do not literally contradict the rule of silence, they may strike at the heart of recollection. For they convey the thoughts, the voices, the entertainments of the world in package form into the interior of the monastery. It would be useless to forgo the real world if one preserved a hunger for it through a daily diet on its image.

Chapter VII Humility

Brothers, Holy Scripture cries aloud to us, saying, 'Whoever exalts himself will be humbled, and he who humbles himself will be exalted.'[1] When it says this it is teaching that all exaltation is a kind of pride. And the prophet shows that he himself was on his guard against it, when he said, 'Lord, my heart has no lofty ambitions, my eyes do not look too high; I am not concerned with great affairs, or marvels beyond my scope.'[2] Why thus? 'If I did not think humbly, but exalted my soul, as a child on the mother's breast is weaned, so did you treat my soul.'[3] Jan. 25 May 26 Sept. 25

So, brothers, if we wish to reach the highest peak of humility, and to arrive quickly at that state of heavenly exaltation which is attained in the present life through humility, then that ladder which appeared to Jacob in his dream, on which he saw angels going up and down, must be set up, so that we may mount by our own actions. Certainly that going down and up is to be understood by us in the sense that we go down through pride and up through humility. The ladder itself that is set up is our life in this world, and the setting up is effected by the Lord in the humbled heart. The sides of the ladder we call the body and soul, and in them the divine call inserts the diverse rungs of humility and (interior) discipline. Jan. 26 May 27 Sept. 26

The first step of humility, then, is for a man to set the fear of God always before his eyes, and utterly to avoid forgetfulness. He must always remember all Jan. 27 May 28 Sept. 27

---

[1] Lk 18:14 [2] Ps 130:1 [3] ibid. 2

God's commandments, and constantly turn over in his heart how hell will burn those who despise him by their sins, and how eternal life has been prepared for those who fear him. At every moment a man must be on his guard against sins and vices—vices of thought, word, hand, foot or self-will, and also against the desires of the flesh. He must recognise that he is at every hour in the sight of God in heaven, and that his actions are everywhere visible to the divine eyes of God, and are being reported to God by the angels from moment to moment. This is made clear to us by the prophet when he shows us that God is always present in our thoughts, 'God examines', he says, 'the heart and the mind.' [4] And also, 'The Lord knows exactly how men think.' [5] And yet again, 'You read my thoughts from far away' [6] and 'Even the thought of man shall praise you.' [7] In order then to keep his perverse thoughts under careful control, the profitable brother should repeat in his heart, 'Then I shall be spotless in his sight, if I keep myself in check against my sinfulness.' [8]

Jan. 28
May 29
Sept. 28
Scripture, indeed, forbids us to do our own wills saying to us, 'Turn away from your will.' [9] Moreover, we ask God in our prayers that his will may be done in us. Truly then we are taught not to do our own will, when we accept the warning of Scripture, 'There are ways which seem right to a man, but in the end they plunge him into the depth of hell,' [10] and also when we tremble at what is said of the indifferent, 'They are corrupt and depraved in their pleasures.' [11] Indeed in what concerns the desires of the flesh, we must believe that God is ever present to us, even as the prophet says,

---

[4] Ps 7:10 [5] Ps 93:11 [6] Ps 138:3 [7] Ps 75:11 [8] Ps 17:24 [9] Sir 18:30 [10] Pr 16:25 [11] Ps 13:1

'All my desires are known to you.' [12]

We must, therefore, be on our guard against any evil desire, because death is stationed beside the entrance to delight, as Scripture teaches in the words, 'Do not go after your lusts.' [13] So if the eyes of the Lord are upon the good and the wicked[14] and if the Lord is always looking down from heaven upon the children of men to see if there are any that act wisely and seek after God,[15] and if daily our works are reported to the Lord by the angels assigned to us, then, brethren, we must constantly be on our guard, lest one day God beholds us falling into sin and becoming unprofitable and (although he spare us in this life because he is merciful and waits for our repentance) he should say to us in the hereafter, 'This you did, and I was silent.' [16] Jan. 29 May 30 Sept. 29

The second step of humility is that a man should not love his own will nor take pleasure in carrying out his desires, but rather by his actions imitate the Lord in his saying, 'I came not to do my own will, but that of him who sent me.' [17] And it has been written, 'Self-indulgence brings its penalty, endurance brings forth a crown.' Jan. 30 May 31 Sept. 30

The third step of humility is that for the love of God one should be obedient to a superior in all things, imitating the Lord of whom the Apostle says, 'He was made obedient even unto death.' [18] Jan. 31 June 1 Oct. 1

The fourth step of humility is that, when in the very act of obeying one meets with trials, opposition, and even abuse, a man should, with an uncomplaining spirit, keep a firm grip on patience and as he endures he should neither grow faint nor run away; even as Feb. 1 June 2 Oct. 2

[12] Ps 37:10 [13] Sir 18:30 [14] Pr 15:3 [15] Ps 13:2 [16] Ps 49:21 [17] Jn 6:38 [18] Ph 2:8

Scripture says, 'He who stands firm to the end will be saved,' [19] and again, 'Let your heart take courage and hope in the Lord.' [20] Further, to show us how a faithful man should suffer all things however painful on the Lord's behalf, it gives voice to those who suffer in the words, 'For your sake we are afflicted by death all the day long, and are reckoned as sheep for slaughter.'[21] Yet unmoved through their hope of divine reward they joyfully persevere, saying, 'These are the trials through which we triumph on account of him who has loved us.' [22] And elsewhere Scripture says again, 'You tested us O God; you refined us in the fire as silver is refined; you led us into the net; you laid tribulations on our backs.' [23] And to show that we ought to be under a superior, it continues, 'You have set men over our heads.'[24] Precisely then they patiently fulfil the command of the Lord in these trials and rebuffs, and when they are struck on one cheek they offer the other.[25] When someone takes away their tunic they allow him to take their cloak also. When they are forced to go one mile, they go two; like the Apostle Paul they put up with false brethren, and bless those who curse them.[26]

Feb. 2 June 3 Oct. 3 The fifth step of humility is that a man should in humble confession reveal to his Abbot all the evil thoughts that come into his mind, and any wrongful actions that he has done in secret. In this connection Scripture exhorts us in the words, 'Reveal your course to the Lord, and hope in him,' [27] and again, 'Make confession to the Lord for he is good, and his mercy is everlasting;' [28] and yet again the prophet says, 'I have declared my sin to you, I have not covered up my evil

[19] Mt 10:22 [20] Ps 26:14 [21] Rm 8:36 [22] ibid. 37 [23] Ps 65, 10,11
[24] ibid. 12 [25] Mt 5:39–41 [26] I Co 4:12 [27] Ps 36:5 [28] Ps 105:1

actions; I made this resolve: I will confess my evil deeds to the Lord, and you have forgiven the guilt of my heart.' [29]

The sixth step of humility is that a monk should be Feb. 3
June 4
satisfied with whatever is of lowest value or quality, Oct. 4
and with regard to the tasks laid on him should think of himself as a bad and unworthy workman, repeating to himself the words of the prophet, 'I have been brought to nothing; I have known nothing; I am like a pack-animal before you . . . and yet I am always with you.' [30]

The seventh step of humility is that he should not Feb. 4
June 5
only say in words that he is inferior and less virtuous Oct. 5
than all other men, but that he should really believe it in the depth of his heart, making the same act of humility as the prophet, who says, 'I am a worm and no man; the scorn of mankind, the jest of the people.' [31] 'I have been lifted up, I have been brought down, and reduced to confusion.' [32] And again, 'It is good for me that you have humiliated me, so that I may learn your commandments.' [33]

The eighth step of humility is that a monk should do Feb. 5
June 6
nothing except what is recommended by the common Oct. 6
rule of the monastery and the example of those above him.

The ninth step of humility is that a monk should Feb. 6
June 7
keep his tongue from talking; he should preserve silence Oct. 7
and not speak until he is questioned, for the Scripture teaches that, 'In much talking, one will not escape sin,' [34] and that 'the talkative man is not directed in his life.' [35]

The tenth step of humility is that he should not be Feb. 7
June 8
Oct. 8

---

[29] Ps 31:5 [30] Ps 73:22, 23 [31] Ps 21:7 [32] Ps 87:16 [33] Ps 118:71
[34] Pr 10:19 [35] Ps 139:12

ready and quick to laughter, for it is written, 'The fool raises his voice in laughter.' [36]

Feb. 8
June 9
Oct. 9 The eleventh step of humility is that when a monk speaks, he does so quietly, without laughter, with humility, with restraint, making use of few words and reasonable ones, as it is written, 'The wise man becomes known for his few words.'

Feb. 9
June 10
Oct. 10 The twelfth step of humility is not only that a monk should be humble of heart, but also that his humility should be apparent in his physical appearance to those who see him. That is to say: whether he is at the work of God, in the oratory, in the monastery, in the garden, on the road, in the field or anywhere else, whether sitting, walking or standing, he should always have his head bowed, his eyes fixed on the ground, and should at every moment be considering his guilt for his sins and thinking that he is even now being presented for the dread judgement. He should always be saying in his heart what the tax-gatherer in the Gospel said with downcast eyes, 'Lord, sinner as I am, I am not worthy to raise my eyes to heaven;'[37] or again with the prophet, 'I am bowed down and humbled at all times.' [38]

Thus when all these steps of humility have been climbed, the monk will soon reach that love of God which, being perfect, drives out all fear.[39] Through this love all the practices which before he kept somewhat fearfully, he now begins to keep effortlessly and naturally and habitually, influenced now not by any fear of hell but by the force of long practice, and the very delight he experiences in virtue. These things the Lord, working through his Holy Spirit, will deign to show in

---

[36] Sir 21:23 [37] cf. Lk 18:13 [38] Ps 118:107 [39] I Jn 4:18

his workman, when he has been purified from vice and sin.

Humility

The chapter opens with the emphatic statement that *Holy Scripture cries aloud* to draw our attention to this theme. It cried so loudly to St Benedict that quotations from Scripture tumble throughout on one another's heels. From the Psalms alone twenty-three citations bear witness to the thoughts he drew from his prayer; and there are many others. There are allusions to the parable of the Pharisee and the publican at the beginning and more obviously at the end; it shows in cameo what is wanted and what is not wanted.

The doctrine which this massive citation from Holy Writ is intended to support is this: in the relationship between God and man, humility is the primary quality with which man must come into the presence of God. There is no other foundation. Throughout the Rule are found regulations providing for the practice of humility by all in the household of God. Here the theory is explained.

Soul and body, each has its contribution to make to life, rather as two sides are necessary to hold a ladder together, and the human life formed by these two is likened to a ladder pointed heavenwards. But only the Lord can do this orientating or erecting, and he requires and gives a humble heart. *The divine call* invites us to mount heavenwards by climbing the steps of humility, which mark the stages of purgation for the soul.

They are understood thus:

1 The first step (it is rather like a broad pedestal) requires the monk to aim at a state of recollection, in which he becomes aware that God is ever present. '*You read my thoughts from far away*,' and these thoughts are not always naturally in conformity with the divine good pleasure; unworthy thoughts naturally rise up in us—false desires, carnal thoughts, worldly thoughts, all the contents of a disorientated mind. The remedy against them is to keep always in one's mind, with a certain reverential fear, that God is present at all times. If we give way to these thoughts we become *useless* and unprofitable servants (cf. the parable of the ten talents); a good servant is also a useful servant engaged in his master's business.

To avoid forgetfulness utterly: we are sailing in the opposite direction to the world's maxim: 'Get away from it all! Find a place in which to forget!'

2 We succeed in nothing by ourselves, and so the second step brings us into closer association with Christ. We have been warned to keep a watch on our thoughts; it is not enough. Good thoughts have to be accompanied by *good actions*. These are possible only if we accept our position as a follower of Christ, who said '*I came not to do my own will . . .*' We are led then to the choice: my own will or the following of Christ in his obedience. We must beware of the idea—based on a distrust of God, or on false teaching—that the divine will is to be associated with the disagreeable. Quite the reverse.

3 This consideration, being applied in the concrete, leads the monk to the third step, to accept obedience to a man as Christ's representative. This, too, was the way that Christ lived.

4 It may seem strange, but the next stage is not that gentle peace (which is the world's kindliest idea of cloistered life) but a turbulent sea of troubles. As it were from nowhere arise difficulties, contradictions—even injustices. Christ's mission did not prove to be a smooth path, and in some way or other his follower finds himself also on a bumpy road. But he is not sad. For, trusting God, the monk perseveres *with joy*, experiencing that these are the very *trials through which we triumph* on account of him who loved us. If he finds that his path involves suffering after the manner of Christ's suffering, he finds triumph, too, through the power of Christ's resurrection. There is, however, this significant difference: he is aware that his suffering is due to him for his sinfulness and is related to his weakness, whereas when he touches joy and the knowledge of triumph, this is something made over to him by Christ. This is the process by which he is being caught up into the Paschal Mystery.

5 It is not important in these trials to conduct a successful defence of oneself. Alas, our poor human nature thinks self-defence to be all important! On the contrary it is the elimination of self-esteem, and natural self-love and every root of disorientation from God that is important. Deep-lying, if apparently unaggressive, defects are brought to the surface by tribulation. Let them be confessed to God. But it is better still if they are confessed to him who stands in the place of Christ, and does so for the very purpose of helping, guarding and strengthening him who has reached this critical stage. (How great is the Abbot's responsibility at this moment; how much he will depend on the charismatic gift implied in his name! This is the moment of service.)

6 The descent continues. The workman sees his worthlessness and unprofitableness. He must be content with the lowest wage, the worst of everything. He has earned no better. Yet he murmurs ever in his heart: Lord, *I am truly with you.* He knows deep down that he is being purified, not rejected. He knows that this implies the sustaining nearness of God.

The few words that are quoted from Psalm 72, are just enough to indicate where to look for the whole message. Here (in the Grail version) is some more of it:

> I was stupid. I did not understand,
> No better than a beast in your sight.
> Yet I was always in your presence,
> You were holding me by your right hand.
> You will guide me by your counsel,
> And so you will lead me to glory . . .
> My body and my heart faint for joy;
> God is my possession for ever. (vv. 22–24,26)

7 The descent goes lower yet. Not only is the monk conscious of the failure of his spiritual endeavours, but the panorama of his life shows him to be a failure in comparison with the person he feels he should have been. He has achieved nothing except to find out that what is born of flesh is flesh. This is the lowest point, at which the 'old self' gives up and dies. If it is genuine and not a pretence such death is bound to be painful. Yet the monk is not deserted. He knows in his heart that this is not rejection, but a learning process. He lives with the thought: *It is good for me that you have humiliated me, so that I may learn* (that I depend totally on you to be able to walk in the way of) *your commandments.* St Peter learnt this in his fall; every servant of God is invited to learn it one way or another.

8 Here comes a warning to the monk that no special attempt is to be made to salvage his reputation or good standing. Let him not seek to make an impression on his world by some noteworthy achievement. Let him be content to pass unnoticed, doing only what the common rule calls for. It is enough. The interior annihilation is not to be compensated for by any prowess in the way of austerities, long fasts, or vigils in prayer. Any attempt, inspired by such a motive, to improve his position, will be an error.

9, 10, 11 And let him be silent also, and quiet and gentle in his relations with his brethren. If he is still assertive and heated in his speech, he has still a lot to learn. Nor should he seek a way out by the path of loud laughter; it is apt to be a sign of the non-learner (*the fool*).

12 If he ends this process feeling like the publican in the temple whose prayer was a *bowed head* and the words *God be merciful to me a sinner*,[40] and this becomes a permanent disposition, accompanying him everywhere, then he is very near experiencing the touch of the Lord, which completes and perfects in him the love that has propelled him along this path with its narrowness and occasional stoniness. Where before love and fear mingled in him, now love and joy leave no room for fear. It is not that he achieves this by conquest; he reaches it by surrender through humility. He has accepted the path of lowliness and purification, he has willed to tread the path his Master trod, and now the Lord acting through the power of his Spirit wills to demonstrate the divine goodness to him by giving that *delight in virtue*, which means that law as such no longer constrains him, for he is led onwards now by the gentle promptings of the Holy Spirit.

Two practical points may be noted here:

First, a spiritual map such as the Rule traces here is based on experience, but it is certain that God leads each person in an individual way, such as is suited to him.

Secondly, the transformation of the spiritual life described in the last few lines is not to be understood as if there were first one long Dark Night and then the brilliance of an unending day. In fact this is the ontological sequence; chronologically, joy and suffering, purification and the working of the power of the Spirit are mingled as the days go by, as God sees best for each of us.

The monastic life is not then just a routine, not even just a sanctifying routine. As with other types of life there is indeed routine, but beneath the routine of the monastic life a pilgrimage is going on, a dynamic conversion is expected to take place. The

---

[40] Lk 18:13

monk begins by answering the divine call. He enters on a lifelong programme marked indeed by purification from his defects, but consisting essentially of an entry in spirit into the Paschal Mystery of Christ's death and resurrection, accepting suffering, knowing triumph, through the action of the Holy Spirit. The observances detailed elsewhere have for object the facilitation of this ascent into the freedom of the children of God.

One further point: Does God then insist on a lot of suffering before he grants the reward? Strictly speaking, God who is all love and compassion is not the author of human suffering. But the soul, responsive to the divine call, runs towards him, and finds itself impeded, as it runs, by exterior and interior fetters. It is the shedding of these fetters which is painful; the difficulty with which it is accomplished depends largely on the intensity with which we are in love with these hindrances, and is lessened by the simplicity and generosity with which we trust God and abandon them.

Moreover, it is clear from the examples of the saints that God does allow unmerited sufferings to befall his servants; and that they understand this as a privilege, a giving to them of a share in redeeming the world in union with Christ.

NOTE: This chapter on humility is short in comparison with the numerous themes treated, and is a treatise on the purgative aspect of the spiritual life. A modern writer would require many pages to teach this ascesis, but it is characteristic of the ancients to say to their disciple, 'Here is a text of Scripture; meditate on it; when you are ready, you can come back for another.' So St Benedict is largely content to make use of his organised texts of Scripture to illustrate the path to God. Hence his chapter will come to life in so far as we are prepared to allow his quotations from Scripture to talk to us seriously.

The next section, Chapters VIII–XIX, is devoted to the organisation of the Divine Office. We shall, however, find nothing resembling a treatise on liturgy. The Rule aims:

To provide a timetable of the Divine Office with seasonal adjustments
To set up a structure of the Office to be used with this programme
To provide safeguards for its punctual and worthy performance.

These chapters controlled the Divine Office for many centuries until the present day. In some monasteries they still do; there has, however, been a great deal of reorganisation in recent years, aimed at bringing in 'a new look'.

The commentary will touch mainly on the spiritual values indicated in these chapters.

Chapter VIII The Divine Office at Night

Having considered what is reasonable we lay down that during the winter (that is from 1 November till Easter) the time of rising will be the eighth hour of the night. Thus they may sleep for a while after midnight and get up after digestion has been completed. The time that is left after Matins is to be used for further study by the brethren whose knowledge of the Psalter or of the readings is incomplete. From Easter till the aforesaid 1 November, the hour of rising should be so determined that there is a short interval after Matins, during which the brethren can go out for the necessities of nature. Lauds which follow are to be said as dawn is breaking.

Feb. 10
June 11
Oct. 11

The Time of the Night Office

1 The main point of the chapter is to settle the hour of the Night Office. It was significant to have a Night Office, since Christ said 'Watch and pray' (cf. also Chapter XVI). But the Rule does not set out to demand a heavy austerity; hence adequate hours of sleep are provided beforehand—as much indeed as a man would need. The 'alternative society' was in a position to make an entirely independent use of the twenty-four hours.

2 It was important to begin Lauds at break of day. New light was a call to new thanksgiving to God the giver of light, and the time to honour his Son, who was thought of as the world's true Dawn.

3 A special time is laid down here for the brethren to study the Psalms. The monk had to learn them by heart since there was no general issue of Psalters, and at the Night Office the main or only lighting was that of the candles at the lectern. The instruction remains significant: those who intend to devote hours to praising God through the Psalms, stand to profit greatly by a genuine voyage of exploration into their meaning. And for this we are given the tools as never before by modern scriptural study.

Chapter IX The Number of Psalms to be said at the Night Office

During the winter period mentioned above, first of all there should be said three times the versicle, 'Lord open my lips, and my mouth will proclaim your praise,'[1] to be followed by Psalm 3 and the *Glory be*; after this Psalm 94 should be chanted with an antiphon, or at least chanted. Then the hymn should follow, and next six Psalms with antiphons. When these are ended and the versicle has been said, the Abbot should pronounce a blessing. Then when all are seated in their stalls, three readings should be read by the brethren in turn from the book on the lectern, and between them three responsories should be sung. Two responsories should be sung without *Glory be*, but after the third reading, the singer should chant the *Glory be*, and when he begins it all should at once rise from their seats in honour and reverence for the Holy Trinity. The books of divine authorship, of both the Old and New Testaments, should be read at Matins, and also the commentaries on them written by well-known and approved Catholic Fathers. After these readings with their responsories another six Psalms should follow; they are to be sung with Alleluia. After these Psalms, there should follow a reading from the Apostle, recited by heart, the versicle, and the prayer of the litany, that is *Lord have mercy*. And so let Matins conclude.

Feb. 11
June 12
Oct. 12

The Order of the Night Office

1 The Night Office began the daily round of prayer and was also

[1] Ps 50:17

the longest hour. Its opening is solemn—a special verse is chanted three times. This was a most ancient custom, and in fact the selected verse preceded the Eighteen Benedictions of the synagogue.

2 Psalm 94 which follows is not so much a prayer to God, as an invitation to the worshippers to 'come in' and set about their task joyfully (v. 1), reverently (v. 6), and penitently (v. 8). The call to spiritual awakening sounded in the Prologue is renewed daily in this Psalm.

3 The Abbot's '*blessing*'; or it could be translated *prayer*. Then follow the readings. There are three movements in every hour of the Divine Office: the prayer of praise (hymn, Psalms), the prayer of petition which comes at the end, and the reading of God's word. Thus we are taught to praise and thank God first, to listen to his message in reverent silence, and also to bring forward our own petitions. These three strands make the Divine Office a complete audience with God.

4 *The Glory be is sung . . .*: Thus the Psalms receive a Christian orientation, and the *honour and reverence* due to the Holy Trinity is practically inculcated.

5 Alleluia: See Chapter XV. The way it was used was very different from present practice.

6 The Litany: Something like our Bidding Prayers. The *Lord have mercy* was the refrain answering each petition.

Chapter X How the Praise of God is to be performed on Summer Nights

From Easter till November the same number of Psalms, as set down above, is to be retained, but on account of the nights' being short, no lessons are to be read from the book. Instead of these three readings, one from the Old Testament is to be recited by heart, followed by a short responsory. All the rest should be carried out as set down above. Thus, never less than twelve Psalms should be said at Matins, not counting the 3rd and 94th. Feb. 12 June 13 Oct. 13

The Night Office in Summer

1 Two characteristics emerge from this chapter: (1) Even as concerns prayer, the programme is closely woven with the cycle of nature. In the age of artificial light inevitably we behave differently. (2) The brethren are not sacrificed to the norms set out in Chapter IX, but the summer programme is shortened to meet their needs and the realities of the situation.

2 The number of twelve Psalms was taken from the Egyptian monks. St Benedict is saying: Reduce the lessons, but not the Psalms.

3 The short lesson from the Old Testament is balanced by one from the New Testament at Lauds.

Chapter XI How Matins are to be carried out on Sundays

Feb. 13 June 14 Oct. 14 On Sundays the hour of rising for Matins should be earlier. In this Office the method is as follows: When the six Psalms and the versicle have been chanted, as we set out above, and all are seated in due order in their stalls, four readings should be read from the book (as we said before) with their responsories, and the *Glory be* is chanted only in the fourth responsory; when he begins it all should rise at once with reverence. After these readings another six Psalms should follow in order with antiphons, as before, and a versicle. After these again four more lessons should be read with responsories, as set out before. Then three canticles from the prophets, as chosen by the Abbot, should be sung with Alleluia. When the verse has been said, the Abbot gives a blessing, and four more lessons are read from the New Testament in the way already described. After the fourth responsory the Abbot intones the hymn *We praise you, O God*; when this is finished the Abbot reads from the Gospel, while all stand in reverential honour. At the end of the reading all reply *Amen*, and next the Abbot begins the hymn *To You Praise is due*, and after the prayer, they begin Lauds. This order of Matins is to be kept on Sundays in both the summer and winter seasons—unless by chance they get up late (which should not happen) and some abridgement of the readings or responsories has to be made. But great care should be taken that this does not happen, but if it does, the person through whose carelessness it has occurred must make adequate satisfaction to God in the oratory.

The Night Office on Sundays

1 The Office is longer, since it is the Lord's Day and work is suspended. There is no need for a distinction between winter and summer. The brethren will either go out for Mass, or if they have a priest, have Mass in their own oratory.

2 There will be a special reading from the Gospel at Matins, making it altogether more solemn than any other hour of the week. It will be surrounded by such ceremony as their way of life permits.

First a hymn of thanksgiving, intoned by the Abbot; then all stand in *reverential honour* while he reads; all will declare their adherence to the message by their acclamation at the end. Then the Abbot intones a hymn of *praise*, before concluding with a prayer that presents the petitions of all. This is the sequence of attitudes in which the reading of the Gospel is enshrined: thanksgiving, reverential honour, acceptance, praise, petition.

3 St Benedict is willing to shorten the Divine Office when necessary (Chapter X), but protests against this happening by chance or carelessness.

Chapter XII How the Solemn Office of Lauds is to be carried out

Feb. 14 June 15 Oct. 15 Lauds on Sunday begin with Psalm 66, chanted continuously without an antiphon. After that, Psalm 50 is chanted with Alleluia. And then Psalm 117 and Psalm 62. Then the canticle *O All you Works of the Lord, Bless the Lord*, and the *Praises*,[1] a reading from the Apocalypse learnt by heart, a responsory, the hymn, the versicle, the canticle from the Gospels, and the litany to form the conclusion.

The Office of Lauds on Sundays

All parts of this carefully composed Office are significant:
1 The Introductory Psalm 66, chosen on account of the verse: *Let your face shed its light upon us*, indicates the solemnity of the hour.

2 Psalm 50: It was customary to begin daily with a penitential prayer.

3 Psalm 117: The Psalm of the Resurrection. (*This is the day which the Lord has made! Let us be glad and rejoice in it!*)

4 Psalm 62: The perfect choice for morning prayer. *O God my God for you do I watch at the break of day* (Vulgate version).

5 The Canticle from Daniel in which all creatures, great and small, high and low, are invited to join us in the praise of God.

6 Psalms 148–150 joined together were known as the *Praises* (Laudes). This usage was then universal in East and West, and continued so until this century.

---

[1] Psalms 148–50

7 The use of Alleluia is continued after Matins because Sunday is the day of the Resurrection.

8 The short lesson came from the Apocalypse; this book celebrates the Victory of the Lamb, who was slain, and whose victory the Church shares.

9 The Canticle from the Gospels was the *Benedictus*; it contained the words: *To give light to those who sit in darkness.*

In the Jewish tradition the darkness of night was associated with trial and sorrow, morning was the hour of deliverance, of God's special favours. The monastic interpretation of this inheritance was to spend part of the night in the prayer of watching, and to treat the arrival of morning as the moment for proclaiming the joy of being redeemed by Christ.

Chapter XIII How Lauds are carried out on ordinary Days

Feb. 15 June 16 Oct. 16 On ordinary days the solemn Office of Lauds is to be carried out as follows: Psalm 66 is to be said without an antiphon, and rather slowly (as on Sunday) so that all may arrive in time for Psalm 50 which is to be chanted with an antiphon. After this, let two more Psalms be chanted, keeping to custom, namely: on Monday 5 and 35, on Tuesday 42 and 56, on Wednesday 63 and 64, on Thursday 87 and 89, on Friday 75 and 91, and on Saturday 142, and the canticle of Deuteronomy, divided into two parts. On each of the other days is sung a canticle from the prophets, as in the Roman Church. The *Praises* follow, and then a single reading from the Apostle to be recited by heart, the responsory, hymn, verse, canticle from the Gospels, and the litany to form the end.

Feb. 16 June 17 Oct. 17 Definitely neither Lauds nor Vespers should finish without the Lord's Prayer being recited at the end by the superior, while all listen. This is on account of the thorns of mutual offence which occur in the course of events; for in this way they are warned by the undertaking contained in the words of the prayer: *Forgive us as we forgive* and may cleanse their hearts from any defect of this kind. In the other Offices only the last part of this prayer is said, so that all may reply, *But deliver us from evil.*

The Office of Lauds on Weekdays

1 During weekdays also special Psalms referring to the hour of daybreak are selected. The lesson is to be from 'the Apostle' or 'an apostle'. Thus the theme will be the redemption wrought by Christ.

2 A notable addition is made to the last chapter. The Our Father is to be recited twice daily by the Abbot. The reason is extremely realistic. In community life it is of experience that hurts are given and received; twice daily then the brethren will listen to the Lord's precept ordering them to forgive, and so they will cleanse their hearts of whatever is lacking in their forgiveness. To forgive is a 'Must' in the Christian way of life.

Chapter XIV How Matins are carried out on Feast Days of Saints

Feb. 17 June 18 Oct. 18 On the feasts of saints and on all solemn days, Matins are to be carried out as we have laid down for Sundays, except that the Psalms, antiphons and readings proper to the day should be said; but the order of the Office should be as previously detailed.

The Night Office on Solemn Days

Feast Days or Solemn Days in honour of the saints were few. On them work would be suspended and there would be Mass. It was then fitting to lengthen the Night Office on the Sunday model; and also that a special selection of Psalms should be made to fit the theme; the antiphons would come out of the Psalms. Appropriate readings could easily be found. No changes seem to have been made in the other hours.

Chapter XV When Alleluia is to be said

From the holy feast of Easter until Pentecost Alleluia should be said throughout the Office both in the Psalms and in the responses. Feb. 18 June 19 Oct. 19

From Pentecost till the beginning of Lent it should be said every night with the second group of Psalms only.

On every Sunday (outside Lent) the canticles of Matins, Lauds, Prime, Terce, Sext and None should be said with Alleluia; but Vespers should be sung with an antiphon.

Except from Easter to Pentecost, responsories are never to be said with Alleluia.

The Seasons of the Alleluia

1 This short chapter shows us how the monastic life was coloured by the thought of the Resurrection. The Rule refers rarely to this central event, but the monks were kept fully aware of it by the alternations in their prayer life, especially through the way they used the Alleluia. The word Hallel-Yah (Praise be to God) is found in the Old Testament at the beginning of certain Psalms. In the Apocalypse the four thunderous chants of triumph of the blessed are introduced by Alleluia. 'Alleluia, victory, and glory and power to our God' (Rv 19). So it passed into Christian prayer.

2 The Rule uses the Alleluia to relate the Divine Office to the Paschal Mystery thus:

(i) On an ordinary day it is heard only (but massively) at that part of the Office which immediately precedes dawn, viz. as an antiphon at the 2nd Nocturn—thus it marks the hour of the Resurrection.[1]

(ii) On the Lord's day it is kept back till the 3rd Nocturn (this

---

[1] Mt 28:1; Jn 20:1

being the appropriate hour on Sunday), and then repeated throughout Lauds and used as the antiphon till None exclusively

(iii) In Paschaltide a whole flood of Alleluias colours the Office. Even the ban on its use at the Night Office is lifted

(iv) In Lent no Alleluia is allowed. It is a time for watching in prayer, for penance, and for preparing for the Easter feast

(v) Except during Paschaltide, the Alleluia should not be used during the responsories of the Night Office, nor those of the day, but kept to the prescribed times.

Chapter XVI How the Work of God is carried out during the Daytime

As the prophet puts it, 'Seven times daily I have praised Feb. 19 June 20
you.'[1] This sacred number of seven will be performed Oct. 20
by us if we carry out the duties of our service at Lauds, Prime, Terce, Sext, None, Vespers and Compline, for it is of these hours of the day that he said, 'Seven times a day I have praised you.' And of the Night Office the same prophet said, 'At midnight I got up to give you praise.'[2] Let us therefore at these times give praise to our Creator 'for his righteous judgements',[3] that is to say at Lauds, Prime, Terce, Sext, None, Vespers and Compline, and at night let us get up to thank him.

The Number of the Day Hours

1 Benedict, being a Westerner, takes the prophet literally, whereas by seven the prophet signified perfection, completion. We have to aim at a day so organised that the number of hours is such as to enable us to live as much as possible in God's presence.
2 The phrase '*Let us give praise . . .*' sums up what these chapters are about. Prayer that is mainly petition stops very short of what prayer should be, and may find itself lacking in vitality. Prayer of atonement is necessary for sinners, and is provided for in the Psalms. But prayer is essentially the praise, adoration and loving worship of our Creator, for what he is, and for his judgements by which he creates, makes and rectifies all things everlastingly. This prayer is eternal; it will never cease; under the illumination of the Holy Spirit it becomes increasingly joyful, as we fulfil ourselves, by fulfilling our primary purpose as the creatures of God's love. Through it we fulfil the command: Praise our God, you servants of his, and all who are great and small revere him, and we join

---

[1] Ps 118:164 [2] ibid:62 [3] ibid:164

'the great crowd like the sound of the ocean or a great roar of thunder answering Alleluia! Let us be glad and joyful and give praise to God because this is the time of the marriage of the Lamb';[4] it is the time of the celebration of *God's righteous judgements*.

3 The celebration of the Divine Office is not always easy; it may be felt at times as demanding, even burdensome, and this is our human condition. To be filled with the spirit of praising God is in itself a gift to be sought as the key to other gifts. The vocal praises of God have to be continued in interior prayer, which is not only communication of the soul with God, but also a continuation of this praise in a deep silent way.

[4] Rv 19:5–7

Chapter XVII How many Psalms are to be said at these Hours

The order of the Psalmody at Matins and Lauds has already been dealt with; now we must consider the remaining hours. At Prime three Psalms should be said, separately, and not under one *Glory be*. The hymn is sung after the versicle, *O God Come to my aid*,[1] before beginning the Psalms. When the three Psalms are finished there should be one lesson, a versicle, *Lord have mercy* and the concluding prayers. The Offices of Terce, Sext and None are to be carried out in the same way, thus: the opening verse, the hymn of the hour, the three Psalms, a reading and verse, *Lord have mercy* and the concluding prayers. If the community is large enough antiphons should be used; otherwise the Psalms are sung straight through. Feb. 20 June 21 Oct. 21

For the evening prayer meeting four Psalms with antiphons will be enough. After them a lesson should be recited, then a responsory, a hymn, a versicle, a canticle from the Gospels, the litany and the Lord's prayer at the end.

For Compline the recitation of three Psalms, said straight through without an antiphon, is enough. After these there will be the hymn proper to this hour, a lesson, a versicle, *Lord have mercy*, and the blessing at the end.

The Structure of the Day Hours

In this chapter we may note three points:

1 There is consideration for the human side of life: antiphons will

[1] Ps 69:1

be used at these Offices only if numbers are adequate. For when antiphons (or Alleluia) were intercalated with the Psalms this made the Office longer.

2 The Verse *O God come to my aid* makes its appearance here as an introduction for the minor hours.

It prompted Cassian to write one of his most inspiring pages. Prayer, he teaches, tends to greater simplicity and unity. If the words of this verse are repeated throughout the day – at work, in temptation, in physical weakness, at reading etc., they lead to a continuous state of prayer, and so to contemplation.

'This thought in your heart may be to you a saving formula and not only keep you unharmed by all attacks of devils, but also purify you from all faults and earthly stains, and lead you to that invisible and celestial contemplation, and carry you to that ineffable flow of prayer of which so few have any experience.' [2]

3 Hymns played only a minor part in the Office, but they had the effect of marking the time of day. In this way they gave each hour its special colour.

---

[2] Coll X,10. Cited from *John Cassian* by Owen Chadwick

Chapter XVIII In what Order the Psalms should be said

Feb. 21 June 22 Oct. 22

First should be said the verse: *God come to my aid, Lord make haste to help me*, and *Glory be*; then the hymn of the hour.

Then at Prime on Sunday are to be said four stanzas of Psalm 118; at the remaining hours, namely Terce, Sext and None, three stanzas of the same Psalm are to be said.

At Prime on Monday three Psalms, namely 1, 2 and 6 are to be said, and so on each day at Prime up to Psalm 19, continuing till Sunday (exclusively); but note that Psalms 9 and 17 are to be divided into two parts. In this way the Sunday Matins will always begin with Psalm 20.

Feb. 22 June 23 Oct. 23

At Terce, Sext and None on Monday are to be said the nine remaining stanzas of Psalm 118, three at each hour. Psalm 118 is thus finished on two days, Sunday and Monday; on Tuesday three Psalms are to be chanted at each of Terce, Sext and None, from 119 to 127. And these Psalms are to be repeated daily at the same hours until Sunday; but the arrangement of hymns, readings and verses is to follow the same pattern daily, and on Sunday a new beginning should be made with Psalm 118.

Feb. 23 June 24 Oct. 24

Vespers are to be sung each day with four Psalms, beginning with Psalm 109 and ending with Psalm 147, but excluding those which are assigned to other hours, namely Psalms 117–27, 133 and 142; the rest are all to be said at Vespers. Since, however, there are three Psalms too few, the longer Psalms of those just mentioned, namely 138, 143, 144 are to be divided into two. On the other hand Psalm 116, being very short, is to be joined with 115.

This covers the order of the Psalms for Vespers: all the other items, namely the reading, responsory, hymn, versicle and canticle, are to be performed as we have laid down above. At Compline the same Psalms are to be repeated daily, namely 4, 90 and 133.

Feb. 24 (in L.Yr.) June 25 Oct. 25

This settles the order of the Psalms during the day: all the remaining Psalms are to be divided equally into the seven vigils of the night; twelve are to be allotted to each night, but dividing the Psalms of greater length. Nevertheless, we emphasise that if anyone is dissatisfied with this arrangement of the Psalms, he is to organise them otherwise as he finds better; he should, however, see to it that the Psalter with its full number of a hundred and fifty Psalms be recited every week, starting anew from vigils of the Lord's Day. For monks who in the course of a week sing less than the Psalter with its usual canticles manifest a service too slothful for their dedicated state, since we read that our holy Fathers vigorously completed in a single day what it is to be hoped we who are tepid may accomplish in a whole week.

The Arrangement of the Psalter

1 The previous chapters have provided the structure of the Divine Office—the texts have been left free. Occasionally this is underlined (the Abbot chooses the canticles from the prophets, cf. Chapter XI), for freedom implies responsibility, and responsibility means thinking about things and stimulates interest. The fixation of the texts for reading which came in later was alien to the spirit of the Rule, and must have done much harm. The only texts regulated in detail are the Psalms, for which this chapter provides the order. But it does do it with great openness of mind, insisting that if any one can do better will they please do so. It is not, then, contrary to the mind of St Benedict if, with all the wealth of knowledge at our disposal today, we have other arrangements of the Psalter.

2 By the arrangement of the Rule, apart from a few especially chosen ones, the great majority of Psalms are to be recited in their numerical order. When this does not fit the desired quantity, they may be divided or even spaced over two days. The implication is that the Psalms were seen mainly as material for meditation, and as stimulating the lifting of the mind to God. With certain exceptions (cf. Chapter XII) there is not much concern for the liturgical value of each Psalm. We tend to take the opposite point of view, and no doubt this is the result of greater erudition and of our study of the liturgy. The perfect liturgy will no doubt combine both aspects and it seems reasonable to suppose that St Benedict would want us to continue our search into the creation of the most perfect possible prayer in our own times, with room for meditation and repentance, and exuberant praise, and a skilful choice of reading matter. This implies a choice and use of scriptural texts, including the Psalms, such as to draw from them their fullest liturgical and meditative value.

3 The little phrase the *service of their dedicated state* (lit. the service of their devotion) is worthy of reflection. For the monk leaves behind some of the burdens of ordinary human life to embrace a special work. So the chapter ends with a warning against tepidity and sloth, assuming realistically enough that the monks will be tempted to reduce the amount of service or worship to which their state commits them.

4 Compline was said apparently wherever they were gathered together, and could be said entirely without light. The addition of an antiphon in honour of Our Lady came in during Cistercian times.

Chapter XIX Recollection in chanting

Feb. 24 (or 25) June 26 Oct. 26

We believe that God is present everywhere, and that the eyes of the Lord are in every place, keeping watch on the good and the bad;[1] but most of all should we believe this without any shadow of doubt, when we are engaged in the work of God. We should therefore always be mindful of the prophet's words, 'Serve the Lord with fear.'[2] And again, 'Sing wisely.'[3] And yet again, 'In the sight of the angels I will sing to you.'[4] We must therefore consider how we should behave in the sight of the Divine Majesty and his Angels, and as we sing our Psalms let us see to it that our mind is in harmony with our voice.

Behaviour at the Divine Office

1 All has been said about the hours, the structure, the content of the Divine Office; one point remains, an important one: the control of one's internal dispositions. Physical presence can be legislated for; mental presence has to be cultivated. How is that done?

Fundamentally, we must learn to strengthen our belief that God is present everywhere into an attention to his presence with us when we come together to address him in person. 'The essential point of a theology of the liturgy is that we must believe when we participate in the Divine Office that the Lord is present, because he is praying in and through us.'[5] It is not enough to hold this as a principle, it is a habit that calls for cultivation. The result may be called recollection.

2 The Rule reinforces this fundamental thought with a reminder that the angels are also witnesses of our prayer.

3 And further it reminds us: *Sing wisely*. How foolish to spend

---

[1] Pr 15:3 [2] Ps 2:11 [3] Ps 46:8 [4] Ps 137:2 [5] Adrian Nocent

long hours in so serious a task, and yet fail to attend to it! How unwise to allow our times of sacred interview to pass in blankness and boredom!

4 *Let our mind be in harmony . . .*: There are no statistics for distractions. But without the positive and deliberate formation of a good habit, it is certain that the mind will be mainly occupied with something else; intellectual work, the problems of one's job, what I ought to have said to so-and-so, the news of the day . . . Something indeed may remain of profit—the fact of our will to pray shown by our very presence in choir, itself a testimony of fidelity to our consecration . . . no doubt the angels will find something to record of our prayerfulness . . . but how much of spiritual growth, of enlightenment, of renewed fervour, of contact with God is lost, if our mind is simply elsewhere?

5 The use of our own language certainly helps us to keep our mind on what we are saying (and this was the situation which the Rule takes for granted). But sometimes it underlines the divergence between what the psalmist is saying and our own personal attitudes, for example the psalmist's attitude to his enemies. In their use of the Psalms the ancients distinguished four meanings: (1) the literal; (2) the moral, that is, the immediate moral lesson conveyed; (3) the prophetic: this meant that the words were interpreted in terms of the New Testament, or shown as fulfilled by Christ; (4) the anagogic: this meant those higher and more spiritual meanings which the Spirit of God revealed to the monk at prayer. The Spirit taught him a deeper understanding than he would otherwise reach.

Chapter XX Reverence at Prayer

Feb. 25 (or 26) June 27 Oct. 27

If we wish to bring anything to the attention of powerful men, it is only with humility and reverence that we dare to do so. How much more then should we present our supplications to the Lord God of all things with complete humility and devout purity of mind. Indeed we must grasp that it is not by using many words[1] that we shall get our prayers answered, but by purity of heart and repentance with tears. Prayer, therefore, should be short and pure, unless on occasion it be drawn out by the feeling of the inspiration of divine grace. In community, however, the prayer should be kept quite short, and when the superior gives the sign all should rise together.

Reverence at Prayer

1 This short chapter refers to personal prayer whether it be part of a community act or otherwise; it refers rather to the prayer of petition than the prayer of praise, thus completing its teaching by dealing with another aspect of the office of prayer.

2 Unusually for a doctrinal chapter, St Benedict does not quote Scripture, but makes a direct appeal to our common sense. You want your petitions to be heard do you? Well then, this is how things work on a human level. So we are given two guide-lines: (1) We must pray in all humility; (2) A show of humility is not enough: we must keep our mind on the job, we must pray with purity of heart and mind. This phrase seems to refer in the first place to the avoidance of distractions, but means also the elimination of impure motives, such as self-interest, or pride, or a reliance on good works, or much speaking. All such things affect the purity of a prayer.

---

[1] Mt 6:7

3 The sentence beginning: *Indeed we must grasp . . .* implies experience (is there not here an allusion to that gift of faith which is a special gift of the Spirit?). It insists on two things: purity of heart and repentance or the compunction of tears. The former implies a prayer that is not self-interested; it begins with the inspiration of God, goes out to him and returns from him replete with the blessing implored.

Tears of compunction,[2] another sign, referred to several times in the Rule, proceed from a knowledge of unworthiness to be heard by God, combined with a loving faith that knows that the divine goodness is stretching out to receive and accept the prayer. The Spirit of God makes himself felt in a mingling of contrition, faith, trust and wonder—for which tears rather than words are the human expression.

4 It would be foolish to end a colloquy with God when it is flowing freely under the *inspiration of divine grace*. But when this is not the case, and it is unlikely to be so for a whole community simultaneously, St Benedict would have the prayer short and concentrated. We must remember that his Divine Office was already a long prayer with a meditative quality, and the kind of community prayer referred to in this chapter came at the end of the hour.[3]

---

[2] In Ch. 7 ('Tears and Enlightenment') of his book *Inward Stillness* Fr George Maloney SJ gives the patristic teaching on this theme

[3] cf. St Gregory, *Dialogues*: II, 4

Chapter XXI Of the Deans of the Monastery

Feb. 26 (or 27) June 28 Oct. 28

If the community is rather large, brethren of good reputation and holy way of life should be selected from among them and appointed deans. They are to exercise care over their deaneries in all respect according to the commandments of God and the instructions of their Abbot. They should be chosen as deans who are such that the Abbot may be able to share his burdens with them with confidence. They should not be chosen according to seniority but for their merits and their wisdom in teaching. And if any of these deans, becoming inflated with some form of pride, be found worthy of rebuke, he is to be corrected, once, twice, indeed three times; but if he will not amend, he should be removed and another who is worthy should be substituted for him. And we lay down the same procedure for the Prior of the Monastery.

The Deans of the Monastery

1 This chapter completes the structure of the house of God, of which the foundations were laid in Ch. II and III; the final word, however, comes only in Ch. LXV. At Subiaco St Benedict had founded twelve small monasteries each under its own superior, while retaining a general control himself. He did not repeat this plan after transferring himself to Monte Cassino, but still seems to have kept it in mind. Hence the legislation of this chapter lays down that when numbers justify it, the Abbot shall divide the community into sections under deans, and delegate responsibilities to them. These officials are not the same as the councillors of Ch. III. In a later chapter (LXV) he will agree to the institution of a Prior, and this system was the one that prevailed.

2 The chapter remains significant since the Abbot still needs to *share his burdens* with a number of officials, who will carry grave responsibilities for the welfare of the brethren, and on whose loyalty and good judgement he must rely. The social concern shown by such officials (whether known as deans or not) is an all-important factor in the life of the family, as well as contributing to the upholding of monastic discipline.

3 *Brethren of good reputation:* A more literal translation would be *of good testimony*. For the monk is called by his life to testify to the true nature of Christian life. Only those who do this by their *holy way of life* are suitable for the position of dean. The task of the monastery is to give a yet more powerful testimony to the value of Christian living, through their corporate practice of Christ's teachings. The collectivity which is the monastery amplifies the small voice of each individual's contribution.

Chapter XXII How the Monks should sleep

Feb. 27 (or 28) June 29 Oct. 29 The brethren are to sleep each in a single bed. These beds are assigned to them in order according to the length of their monastic life, subject to the Abbot's discretion. If it is possible, all should sleep in one place, but if their numbers do not permit this, they should take their rest by tens or twenties with the seniors who are entrusted with their care. A candle should burn continuously in this room till morning. They should sleep clothed, girt with girdles or cords, but not with their knives at their sides as they sleep, for fear that a brother should be wounded while asleep. And so let the monks be always ready, and when the signal is given, they should get up without delay and make haste to arrive first for the Work of God, but in a gentle and orderly way. The younger brethren should not have their beds together, but dispersed among the seniors. When they get up for the Work of God they may quietly encourage one another since the sleepy are given to making excuses.

The Dormitory

As the Rule took the Night Office as its starting point for the regulation of the whole course of prayer, so it takes the regulations for the night as the starting point for the legislation running through the whole day. A chapter such as this, while full of interesting information for the social customs and arrangements of another age,[1] has relatively little application to our own times. But the nature of the instructions is of interest.

---

[1] cf. *The Rule of St Benedict*, edited by Justin McCann, notes 44, 55, Burns and Oates, 1952

The combination of consideration for human needs and discipline which is a feature of 'the alternative society' shows itself here. On the one hand: a certain standard of furnishing, adequate hours of sleep (cf. Ch. VIII), a modest light burning throughout the night; and although the warning against taking a knife to bed with you is merely quaint to us, it is evidently a human thought, based on experience. On the other hand, discipline is not forgotten; all are to sleep, if possible, in one place, with seniors in charge.

Human also, and by no means dated, is the recognition that at the hour of rising, the will-power of some is at its lowest. Discreetly then, silence may be broken to encourage us. We may note, too, that a certain promptness and eagerness to return to the Divine Service is inculcated. It is a sign of the interior life within us.

The theme passes to the penal code of the alternative society. To some these chapters will seem not merely a witness to a harder age, but also testimony to a more disagreeable one. They may constitute a black mark against St Benedict as a spiritual teacher making him seem not merely dated, but also heavy handed. Before examining this particular code let us note:

(i) When civilisation progresses cruder penalties die out as unnecessary, and are therefore to be rejected

(ii) Civilisation is not to be identified with the permissiveness of society. A permissive society is one which, for want of conviction in the head or members, sustains as few principles as possible

(iii) To have laws and to defend them by sanctions is in itself a sign of a vigorous society that believes in its way of life.

These chapters concern the defences of the monastic society. The most severe penalty it knew was to expel a member.

Chapter XXIII Excommunication for Faults

Feb. 28 (or 29) June 30 Oct. 30

If any brother is found to be contumacious or disobedient or arrogant or a grumbler or one who sets himself up against some point of the Holy Rule or despises the ordinances of his seniors, he is to be warned privately once or twice, according to our Lord's command,[1] by his superiors. If he does not amend his ways, then he should be publicly rebuked before all. If he still does not improve let him undergo excommunication, if he understands the nature of this punishment. If, however, he is stubborn, he must undergo corporal punishment.

How Excommunication is incurred

1 We tend to think of our sins individualistically as between ourselves and God, or between ourselves and a person—we do not weigh them by their effects on our society. We tend also to divide them simply into mortal sins, meaning grave, and venial sins, meaning trivial. To this rather facile kind of thinking, this chapter gives a jolt. It invites to an examination of conscience on certain sinful states of mind, which are not necessarily to be thought of as mortal sins, but yet are definitely damaging to the spiritual welfare of a community, and therefore serious matters:
Am I contumacious?
Am I disobedient?
Am I proud or arrogant?
Am I a grumbler?
Am I contemptuous of the ruling of those in charge?
Am I living in a state of opposition to the Holy Rule?
(And why, let us ask in passing, is the rule called *holy*? Essentially because for those who profess it, it embodies the form in which

---

[1] Mt 18:15–16

they will keep God's commandments, set down first in Holy Scripture.)

2 The code of correction is set out here, namely (a) private correction (twice), (b) public correction, (c) excommunication; it follows the outline given in the Gospel.[2] Excommunication, however, is only for those who understand what it is about; otherwise physical punishments are more suitable.

3 This chapter is concerned only with faults of some gravity which disturb others. The next chapter does something to clarify this point.

---

[2] Mt 18:15–18; cf. I Co 5:9–13

Chapter XXIV How Excommunication is to be regulated

Mar. 1 July 1 Oct. 31 Excommunication or disciplinary measures should be proportionate to the nature of the fault, and the nature of faults is for the Abbot to judge. If then a brother is found to commit less serious faults he is to be deprived of sharing in the common meal. The rules for one who is thus excluded from the sharing in the common meal will be: he may not intone antiphon or Psalm in the oratory; nor may he read a lesson until he has made satisfaction. He must eat alone after the meal of the brethren. Thus if they eat at the sixth hour, he will eat at the ninth; if they eat at the ninth hour, he will eat in the evening; until having made adequate satisfaction he receives pardon.

The minor Excommunication

Faults can be considered as greater or less. For those that are less the penalties are set down here, but they do not amount to excommunication in the true sense of the word. They are penances to be performed; but the brother is not banished from the community. He may not take part in the common meal, or take a leading part in the Divine Office. The procedure supposes that the rights temporarily lost were appreciated and that the brother is spiritually healthy.

Chapter XXV Very serious Faults

The brother who is guilty of a very serious fault is to Mar. 2 July 2
be suspended from sharing in the meals and also from Nov. 1
the oratory. None of the brethren may associate with him in companionship or conversation. He is to be left alone at the work assigned to him and to remain in penitent grief as he reflects on the terrible sentence of the Apostle. This kind of man is handed over to bodily death, so that his spirit may be saved for the day of the Lord.[1] His food he should take alone in such measure and at such time as the Abbot thinks most suitable for him; nor may he or the food that is given him receive a blessing from anyone who passes by.

The Major Excommunications

This chapter may appear to deal with much the same thing as the last, but is really very different. For it treats of true excommunication, ejection from the whole life of the community, whether at work or prayer or table; and the excommunicated monk and his food and his work go alike unblessed. It is the sentence passed by St Paul on the scandalous Christian at Corinth.

To be cut off from the local church, through which one belongs to Christ's Kingdom, a Kingdom that is strong in his victory over evil, is to fall back, in all one's weakness, into the power of the kingdom of darkness. Clearly it was a remedy applicable only to very serious sins, and suitable only for those who understood what it was about.

---

[1] I Co 5:5

Chapter XXVI Unauthorised Association with the Excommunicated

Mar. 3 July 3 Nov. 2 If any brother, acting without instructions from the Abbot, takes it upon himself to associate with an excommunicated brother in any way, or to talk with him, or send him a message, he must likewise undergo the punishment of excommunication.

Prohibition of associating with the Excommunicated

1 The ruling is out of date, but the point is not. It is a protest against a show of false sympathy or the giving of encouragement to one who has incurred a rebuke or a punishment, by taking his part, when his real need is for penitence of heart, amendment, and a recognition that the superior is doing his duty. Fundamentally such conduct is anti-social.

2 The Rule is silent on the more difficult case of the individual who really does need sympathy or has been misjudged or wrongly accused. No doubt St Benedict would reply: Let the brother who is convinced of this, go privately to the Abbot, and let the Abbot hear patiently whatever representations are made.

3 Sometimes, indeed, an Abbot may be bound to silence concerning his reasons for making a judgement on an individual. He may know about a man's failings, but the knowledge is not general, and it is better for the individual that it should not be. Hence the Abbot is bound to silence, and even to accept the criticism that may follow. It is part of the burden that he carries. The brethren will know and appreciate that he carries such burdens on behalf of all, and each one will be more secure through the knowledge that the Abbot would do as much for him.

Chapter XXVII The Concern the Abbot must have for the Excommunicated

The Abbot should carry out with the deepest concern his responsibility for the brethren who fall into sin, 'for it is not those who are in good health who need a doctor, but those who are sick.'[1] For this reason he should, like a skilful doctor, use every possible remedy; for example he may send *senpectae* (that is, mature and wise brethren) to give unofficial consolation to their wavering brother, and induce him to make humble satisfaction, and give him comfort, 'so that he is not overcome by too much sadness'.[2] And so let it be as the Apostle also says, 'that love is reaffirmed towards him';[3] and everybody is to pray for him. Mar. 4 July 4 Nov. 3

It is indeed very important that the Abbot should show his concern, and make speed to employ his skill and energy, lest he lose one of the sheep entrusted to him. For he must bear in mind that it is the care of sick souls that he has undertaken, not a despotic rule over healthy ones. Moreover, he should fear the threats of the prophet, through whose words God says, 'What you saw to be fat you took, and what was weak you threw away.'[4] And let him copy the loving example of the Good Shepherd who left the ninety-nine sheep on the mountains, and went away to search for the one that had gone astray; and had such pity for its weakness that he deigned to lay it on his own sacred shoulders, and so carry it back to the flock.[5]

---

[1] Mt 9:12 [2] II Co 2:7 [3] ibid:8 [4] Ezk 34:3, 4 [5] Lk 15:4, 5

The Abbot's Concern for the Excommunicated

1 *With the deepest concern:* Rather like a papal encyclical this chapter strikes the note of its message in its opening words. Although it occurs in the middle of the penal code of the Rule, it is not written in that spirit at all. It is a very moving exhortation to the Abbot on the meaning of pastoral care, and being a doctrinal chapter, it abounds in quotations and allusions to Scripture.

Most notably we are in the atmosphere of St Luke's Gospel, Ch. 15, on the recovery of what has been lost. The sinner is not thought of as the enemy, the evil-doer, the repulsive servant of Satan, but as one who is lost or as one who is sick. His sickness makes him a candidate for the doctor; his 'lostness' calls for the search by his owner.

So then two examples prevail: That of the *skilful doctor*, and that set out by our Lord himself, the *Good Shepherd*. These are to be the Abbot's models, and there is no reference to the role of judge and imposer of sanctions. Indeed, ironically, it is the Abbot who is reminded that he is under judgement. He must *make speed*, with all his *skill* and *energy* to make sure that none of his—or rather the Lord's—sheep is lost. He is warned by the prophet, and even told not to be a despot; it almost seems that St Benedict has changed sides, showing more sympathy for the sinful (*delinquentes*) who are still *brethren (fratres)*, than for the Abbot. Yet not entirely so, for the Abbot is to see his role as that of the *Good Shepherd*, which was Christ's preferred description of himself.

Very definitely the brethren have their responsibility too. Every one is called on to pray for the *wavering brother*. This is a matter for the whole community (Ch. XXVIII). But a couple who are mature and experienced and good listeners are to be selected to act as a bridge towards the excommunicated. Thus St Benedict himself makes a breach in the isolation of excommunication. 'Show him', he says, 'this extra love, and it may call out a response in love from him.'

2 Today the excommunicated no longer form part of the population of monasteries. And yet that kindly thought about the oppression (*too much sadness*) of loneliness, may provide food for thought. St Benedict feared that excessive loneliness in his troubles might finally sink a man—a point relevant in any epoch.

Chapter XXVIII The Incorrigible

If any brother who has been often corrected for some fault, and even been excommunicated, does not amend his ways, he must receive harsher punishment, that is to say, he must suffer a beating. But if, even after this, he does not amend or if—which God forbid—he is so filled with pride as to want to defend his actions, then the Abbot must act like a wise doctor. If he has made use of poultices, of the ointments of his counsels, of the remedies of Divine Scripture, if he has come at last to the cautery of excommunication, and the blows of the rod, and if he now sees that his work is unavailing—let him make use of what is still greater: his own prayer combined with that of all the brethren that the Lord to whom nothing is impossible may work the salvation of the sick brother. Mar. 5 July 5 Nov. 4

But if even by this means he is not cured then the Abbot must employ the surgeon's knife, as the Apostle says, 'Drive out the wicked man from among you.' [1] And again, 'If the unfaithful one leaves you, let him go,' [2] for fear that one diseased sheep may infect the whole flock.

The ultimate Penalty of Expulsion

1 Since the correction of faults and the amendment of one's ways form one aim of monastic life, it is normal enough for the Abbot to play a part. This is something positive and helpful, going beyond the mere necessity of dealing with what offends seriously against

---

[1] I Co 5:13 [2] I Co 7:15

the communal standards of the monastery or the laws of God.

2 This chapter, however, takes up the theme of Ch. XXV and adds a point more significant than the detailing of a procedure that is no longer followed. When all else fails, the Abbot is instructed to employ what is greater—communal prayer. This does not mean that prayer for a delinquent is left to the final stage, but that, at the final stage, nothing is left but to pray for a miracle, and that even if the cure of the sick man is beyond human skill, *nothing is impossible to God* . . .

3 . . . and if that fails, then with manifest regret, the Rule adds the last sanction of the penal code: the brother can be a brother no longer; he must be expelled.

Chapter XXIX Whether Brethren who leave should be taken back

If a brother has through his own wrong choice left the monastery and wants to come back again, he must first promise to make amendment for having left, and then let him be taken back in the lowest place as a test of his humility. If he goes away a second time, he may be received back, and even a third time; but after that he must realise that the path of return will not be granted him again.

March 6
July 6
Nov. 5

The Readmittance of Monks who go away

The chapter is short and amiable. It does not treat of the brother who has been finally expelled, but of him who has lost heart, or yielded to temptation, or concluded that he should not go on any longer. He is at fault, since he has taken a vow to persevere, but the Rule knows nothing of imprisonment; so he departs.

But then on the other side of temptation things look different. The brother becomes aware of his loss. Seen close-up the world is less brightly coloured, perhaps more of a jungle too. He longs for the support and love of the fraternity of the house of God. Inside it, he saw faults everywhere, outside it, he perceives the value of the whole.

So he returns and asks for readmission. And what happens? It is just a family situation. Will the family receive him back, and give him a chance to fulfil his broken promises? St Benedict says yes, let them do so; after all the family bond and fraternal love count in the scales; but on the other hand the truant should accept a penalty . . .

And if the situation repeats itself? He may have as many as three chances, and then *let him realise* that this is the end. A kindlier decision could hardly be made.

Chapter XXX How Boys are to be corrected

Mar. 7 July 7 Nov. 6 Disciplinary measures should be appropriate to every age and intelligence: hence when boys or youths or others, incapable of understanding how serious a punishment excommunication is, commit offences, such persons are to suffer additional fasts or painful stripes, so that they may be cured.

The Correction of undeveloped Persons

By comparison with its predecessor this chapter must seem short and gruff. Since boys are no longer admitted to monasteries and excommunication is also dated, we need not dwell on it. And yet how difficult a thing it is to carry out the reasonable basis of all codes—*that disciplinary measures have to fit every age and intelligence.* Undeveloped intelligence rather than age constitutes the problem. For there are those who accept instruction very quickly though they are still young, and others who learn mainly the hard way.

This concludes what is called the penal code of the Rule, although certain points will be added later (Ch. XLIII–XLVI). Essentially it aimed at
(i) the preservation of the monastic standards by the imposition of moderate penances (Ch. XXIV)
(ii) the preservation of the monastic family from scandalous behaviour (Ch. XXV and XXX)
(iii) the cure or healing of the individual (Ch. XXVII–XXIX).
There is no such thing as a perfect penal system since the very concept of punishment implies imperfection, some degree of human failure. We have, however, to distinguish between what would have been seen as normal and compatible with Christian joy and progress, and the sad territory corresponding to real failure. The ultimate aim was to erect barriers to stand between the sinner and his incurring of divine sanctions. For ultimately, God has to have his sanctions, his major excommunication being

referred to in Scripture as hell-fire. The heaviest excommunication of the Rule aimed simply at saving a man from this final loss of his soul.

With Chapter XXXI the Rule turns to the material world of the monk—a world in which men eat and drink, have specific physical needs according to their age or state of health, have responsibilities and work to do. From these chapters we can, if we wish, reconstruct a great deal of their way of life, of their material conditions, etc. We have to take care not to import into this picture of sixth-century monks alterations produced by the evolution of the succeeding ages. At a later date the monks will often live in cloisters of great size and beauty; their Divine Worship will be carried out in the setting of a great church or cathedral; they will become influential, revered, and often learned men, of priestly status; the Abbot will become a prelate, perhaps a magnate, and a power in the land. But at the time of the Rule, all is as yet primitive, humble in quality, seminal.

Therein lies the importance of the Rule for a later century. Nostalgia for an idealised past does not contain the seeds of new life. St Benedict was above all things a realist. What is significant is not a precise reconstruction of the conditions in which he lived, nor of those of the monasteries of subsequent centuries, but how he conceived the household of God vis-à-vis *the world of his time. For a cenobitic community today is equally a household of God* vis-à-vis *the conditions of our own time. Conditions change but, if an institution is to retain its identity, principles do not.*

2
The Administration of the Monastery

Chapter XXXI What Kind of Man the Cellarer of the Monastery should be

As cellarer of the monastery should be chosen from the Mar. 8 July 8
community one who is sound in judgement, mature in Nov. 7
character, sober, not a great eater, not self-important, not turbulent, not harshly spoken, not an off-putter, not wasteful, but a God-fearing man who will be a father to the whole community. He is to have charge of all affairs, but he is not to act without the Abbot's approval, and he must carry out his orders. He must not sadden the brethren. If any brother happens to make an unreasonable demand of him, he should not upset him by showing contempt, but refuse the ill-advised petitioner with reasons modestly presented. He must keep guard over his own soul, always bearing in mind that saying of the Apostle that he who has ministered well gains a good reputation for himself.[1] With all compassion he is to have care for the sick, the children, the guests and the poor, knowing for certain that in the day of judgement he will have to render account for his treatment of them all. He must regard the chattels of the monastery and its whole property as if they were the sacred vessels of the altar. He should neglect nothing. He must neither succumb to avarice nor be a wasteful squanderer of the monastery's goods; but he should conduct all his affairs with prudence and in accordance with the Abbot's instructions.

It is essential that he should have humility and if he Mar. 9 July 9
has nothing material to give, he should at least offer a Nov. 8

[1] I Tm 3:13

kind word of reply, as it is written, 'A good word surpasses the best gift.' [2] He must keep under his own care whatever the Abbot has entrusted to him, but he should not undertake anything the Abbot has forbidden. He must provide the brethren with their allotted quantity of food, without fuss or keeping them waiting, so as not to make for them an occasion of sin, keeping in mind the divine saying about the retribution of him 'who causes one of the little ones to sin'.[3] If the community is rather large, helpers should be given him, so that with their aid he may himself tranquilly perform the office entrusted to him.

Whatever has to be asked for or given should be asked for or given at suitable times, so that no one may be upset or saddened in the household of God.

The Office of the Cellarer

The qualities required in a cellarer demand without question the necessary skills for his job, which has of course become vastly more complicated in our modern world. But the Rule asks for more than this, and the qualities called for here may be grouped under three heads: (i) Maturity, which in the Rule is based on being 'God-fearing', (ii) Self-control, (iii) Fatherliness to the point of compassion for the weak ones.

This chapter contains some of St Benedict's best observations on the application of spiritual principles to the material side of life. For example:

1 *He is to have charge of all . . .*: Thus is established the principle of unity in the economy.

2 *He must not sadden . . .*: He is likely to have to say NO at times, so let him cultivate the art of saying it gently. The one refused should not have grounds for nursing a grudge. Indeed, a cellarer

[2] Sir 18:17 [3] Mt 18:6

who replies harshly sooner or later creates a difficult situation for the Abbot.

3 *He must keep guard on his own soul*: Cellarers are exposed to special temptations, to become worldly or worse, to miss their prayers, to think only in terms of material expediency.

4 And they have a large share in carrying out the monastery's responsibilities towards humanity. The cellarer is especially exhorted to take care of four classes of society who cannot fend for themselves. They are not monks—except some of the sick. They have a broad likeness to what are referred to today as the under-privileged classes. The fullness of humanity is to be shown towards them.

5 *The chattels of the monastery as if . . .: sacred* Is this because they belong to the household of God and so acquire a special character? No doubt this enters in; but more essentially there is here a respect for all created things, all the products of man's labour, all the good things that God has entrusted to the monastery for its use and sustenance. There is a big difference between frugality in the use of human things and contempt for them. For the Rule—as for the psalmist—there is one universe; it all belongs to God, and it is all entrusted to men.

6 *It is essential that he should have humility:* No one is expected to succeed without humility. *Without ostentation or keeping them waiting.* The temptations of officialdom are accurately observed—as is the motive for resisting them.

7 *So that no one may be upset . . .*: This sums up the intention of the whole chapter, and indeed of the whole of St Benedict's social legislation. That some will be upset the legislator knows well (cf. Ch. XIII). But the object of the legislation is to eliminate the occasions, as the object of reciting the Lord's prayer is to counteract the results of such occasions. There will be trials to be met in the pilgrimage to God, but the Rule does not set out to create them, but to teach men how to live together as a Christian family, mindful of one another's peace of mind.

Chapter XXXII The Tools and Goods of the Monastery

Mar. 10 July 10 Nov. 9 With regard to the monastery's material possessions such as tools, clothes, or other articles, the Abbot should put in charge of them brethren whose way of life and character he can trust, and then commit all these things to them, as he thinks best, for safe keeping, and return after use. The Abbot should keep a list of them so that when the brethren succeed one another in the tasks assigned to them he may know what is being handed over or received back. If anyone treats the property of the monastery in a dirty or careless manner, he should be corrected and if he does not amend, he should suffer punishment as laid down in the Rule.

Goods and Chattels

The chapter is short and gives the impression that life was very simple; articles of property are apparently not over-numerous and can be listed. Yet although the instructions are brief, and leave the impression that St Benedict is less concerned with the material than the spiritual, yet they are comprehensive. The main principles are:
(i) All property belongs to the community
(ii) It is wrong to be careless about the monastery's property, which enjoys a certain sacredness (cf. Ch. XXXI). Yet when the property is held in common, it is exposed to neglect, since the instinct to treasure what is our own is no longer at work
(iii) The doctrine that teaches orderliness and care in the handling of material things is reinforced by a practical enactment: special persons shall be chosen and put in charge of them.

The point that they should be such as the Abbot *can trust* is well made. For there are certainly no other grounds on which the head of any institution can rely for his peace of mind. And presumably this also implies some positive training, if only by tradition.

The mention of clothes as being the monastery's property may be noted. When the monk makes his vows his own clothes are taken away from him, and henceforth he is clothed in the clothes of the monastery. This is an indication of the monk's making over his whole person to the service of God in community (cf. Ch. LVII).

Chapter XXXIII Whether Monks may have personal Property

Mar. 11 July 11 Nov. 10 It is of the greatest importance that this vice should be totally eradicated from the monastery. No one may take it upon himself to give or receive anything without the Abbot's permission or to possess anything as his own, anything whatever, books or writing tablets or pen or anything at all; for they are not allowed to retain at their own disposition their own bodies or wills, but they must expect to receive all they need from the Father of the monastery. And so it must not be allowed that anyone should have anything which the Abbot has not approved. Everything should be common to all, as it is written, and no one should call anything his own[1] or treat it as such. But if anyone is found to be entertaining this wicked vice, he should be warned once, and a second time; if he does not amend, he should undergo punishment.

The Importance of common Life

If Ch. XXXII was intended to establish the principle that all items of property, large and small, belong to the monastery, and that therefore the Abbot must concern himself, but not overburden himself, with their care and upkeep, this chapter lays down the correlative principle that nothing belongs to the individual monk.

It is one of the severest tenets of the Rule, one in which St Benedict shows no willingness to temporise and consider what may be allowed to the shortcomings of human nature or the diversities of temperament. It is also one of the hardest to keep.

The words of the opening sentence *that this vice should be totally*

---

[1] Ac 4:32

eradicated from the monastery suggest that St Benedict was thinking in terms of other monasteries in which his Rule might be accepted, and was aware that private property was at least a possibility elsewhere.

We should be wrong if we thought that the insistence of the Rule on this point was a result of a pushing of the doctrine of obedience to its logical conclusion. Although in practice the common life functions through obedience to the Abbot, its basis is something deeper and more sacred. This something was even older than the religious life, though preserved in the Church through the religious life. It was the belief that the fullness of Christian charity was reached through the fullness of sharing all goods in common. Christ himself and his apostles had lived from a common purse.[2] And St Luke tells how the first Christians were so united in heart and soul that no one claimed for his own use anything that he had, as everything they owned was held in common. None of their members was ever in want, as all those who owned land or houses would sell them, and bring the money from them to present it to the Apostles; it was then distributed to any members who might be in need.[3]

This living, then, on property held in common was not just an ascetic exercise; it was not designed to keep any member in want; nor was it an application of the vow of obedience; it was the fulfilment of charity and the rejection of personal advantage over another. That is why any infringement of it was regarded as an attack on the social constitution of the house of God, and worthy of every reprobation. To own property has never been a vice in the Christian Church; it becomes a vice only if you have given a solemn undertaking to the contrary.

Today, when disputes over material gain form such an outstanding feature of our society, is there not a need for monasteries and communities which *manifestly* realise in their way of life this fullness of Christian charity and also bring to the fore that relationship with the underprivileged or needy which St Benedict indicates in Ch. XXXI and elsewhere?

---

[2] Jn 12:6; 13:29 [3] Ac 4:32, 34–5

Chapter XXXIV Whether all should receive equal Shares

Mar. 12
July 12
Nov. 11

It is written, 'Distribution was made to each as he had need.'[1] By this we do not say that favouritism should be shown to persons, far from it, but that infirmities should be allowed for. If some one needs less he should thank God and not be upset; if another needs more he should be humble about his weakness, and not feel important on account of the consideration shown him, and thus all members will be at peace. Above all the bad habit of grumbling must not make its appearance in any word or gesture for any reason whatever. If anyone is found guilty of this, let him pay a heavy penalty.

Consideration of individual Needs

This completes the teaching on common life. It is based likewise on Acts 4, and warns against a common pitfall, namely the conclusion that all should receive the same things. For the principle of distribution is not that all should receive alike, but that all should receive what they need. And in practice this requires a much higher degree of spiritual understanding. Thus the brethren are warned not to impugn the Abbot's motives in granting permissions; or, if they are among those receiving more, not to congratulate themselves, as if they had scored a point, but to react with humility for their infirmity, be it physical, psychological or spiritual. The family, then, is seen as completely human; in it strong and weak are bound together and kept in peace by reacting, with the mutual love and understanding that comes from God's Spirit, to the very inequalities that are innate in their humanity.

If this is not understood there is a danger of common life being practised on a basis of common childishness. That would be particularly abhorrent to our times.

---

[1] Ac 4:35

Chapter XXXV The weekly Servers in the Kitchen

The brethren should serve one another, and no one should be excused from kitchen duty except for sickness or because he is more usefully engaged elsewhere, because through this service the reward of an increase in charity is gained. For the weak, however, help should be provided so that this duty may not cause them dejection. Indeed all should have help according to the size of the community and the location. If the community is rather large the cellarer should be excused from kitchen duty and, as we said before, also those who are engaged in more important tasks. The rest should serve one another in turn with charity. The one who is finishing his week's duty does the washing on the Saturday; he should also wash the towels with which the brethren dry their hands and feet. Moreover, he who is ending his week's service together with him who is about to start should wash the feet of all.[1] The outgoing server must restore the crockery he has made use of, washed and intact to the cellarer, and the cellarer must hand them over to the incomer, for so he may know what he is giving out and what he is getting back. Mar. 13 July 13 Nov. 12

An hour before the meal, the weekly servers may each receive, in addition to the allotted quantity, a drink and some bread, so that at the hour of the meal they may serve their brethren without finding the work heavy or complaining. On solemn days, however, they must wait for the Mass. On Sundays, immediately after May 14 July 14 Nov. 13

[1] cf. Jn 13:15

Lauds, the incoming and outgoing servers should prostrate themselves at the feet of all the brethren in the oratory, and ask to be prayed for. The outgoing server is to say the verse, 'Blessed are you Lord God for you have helped and strengthened me.'[2] When this has been said three times, and he has received a blessing, the incoming server follows and says, 'O God come to my aid, Lord make haste to help me.'[3] And this too is to be repeated three times by all. And so, having received the blessing, he begins his week's duty.

The weekly Servers in the Kitchen

1 The title of the chapter might suggest that it dealt with certain officials; in fact this is not so. It deals with all the brethren as they engage in the task of serving the common meals. All are to take their turn at this task, which is seen as a fraternal service, though the Rule does not actually say that every man should cook. Even in those days that might have brought catastrophe at times, and given occasion for grumbling.

The task seems to have been felt as burdensome; hence the prayer for divine aid at the beginning, the concession of a snack beforehand, and the prayer of thanksgiving made at the end of the week.

The importance of the task is that the brethren are fulfilling the teaching of the Lord: the Son of man came not to be served but to serve.[4] They are then to perform this service *in charity*, knowing that through such acts *the reward of an increase in charity is gained.*

2 Moreover, on Saturday the servers *should wash the feet of all* even as Christ, rising after the Paschal meal, washed the feet of all his disciples,[5] and on Sunday *they prostrate themselves at the feet of all.* By these symbolic actions they assimilated themselves to Christ in the Paschal Mystery and imitated his humility.

The doctrine of St Theodore the Studite (+826) followed this tradition: he taught that monks by their submission to one another

---

[2] Dn 3:28 combined with Ps 85:17 [3] Ps 69:1 [4] Mt 20:28 [5] Jn 13:4–5

imitate Christ, who founded cenobitism when he washed his disciples' feet.

If to teach ourselves by the repetition of such symbolic actions does not now come naturally to us, it is the more necessary that we find our own way of making the kernel of the doctrine our own.

3 St Teresa's saying 'The Lord walks among the pots and pans' is well known. St Benedict never produced a saying as charming as that, but he is also teaching assimilation to Christ through the self-giving involved in the work done in the kitchen, and underlining the significance of the act of service carried out during the brethren's meal.

4 Mass was celebrated on Sundays and festivals. The first reference to this custom occurs here.

Chapter XXXVI Sick Brethren

Mar. 15 July 15 Nov. 14 The care of the sick is to be given priority over everything else, so that they are indeed served as Christ would be served, since he said of himself, 'I was sick and you visited me,' [1] and 'what you did to one of the least, you did to me.' [2] But the sick themselves must realise that it is to pay honour to God that they are being served, and they must not vex their brethren by asking for too much. However, they must be borne with patience, because through them a very ample recompense is merited. Therefore let the Abbot pay the greatest attention so that they suffer no neglect.

For the sick brethren a separate room must be provided and to serve them a brother who is God-fearing, diligent and zealous. The use of baths should be allowed to the sick as often as is desirable, but to the healthy and the young this should not be granted very often. Moreover, the eating of meat should be allowed to the sick who are in a weak condition, but when they are restored to health again, all should abstain from meat as usual. The Abbot must take the greatest care that the sick are not neglected by the cellarer or those who serve them, for whatever is done wrong by his disciples concerns him.

Sick Brethren

1 This little chapter is as good an example as any of St Benedict's approach to human problems. It illustrates also the doctrine run-

---

[1] Mt 25:36 [2] ibid: 40

ning through the Rule that Christ is recognised in diverse ways in all with whom we live or have to do. While no doubt humanity prompts the thought that the sick are to receive special care, it is reinforced by the recognition of the suffering Christ in the person of those who are served.

Nor is the matter left as a thought; it is organised. The Abbot has the overall responsibility, but delegates the work to a suitable brother.

The qualities of the monk are defined; they include, as always, that he be God-fearing; this is the basis of responsible and devout behaviour. Such provisions as the monastery can make are detailed: a special room, such food as is desirable for a sick man, baths as necessary . . . And a reminder is given to the sick that they also must show considerateness for those who care for them.

2 The reason why baths were normally forbidden is that in the ancient world they were associated with the pagan way of life—places of meeting and indulging in loose behaviour and carnality.

Chapter XXXVII Old Men and Children

Mar. 16 July 16 Nov. 15 Although human nature itself is drawn to feel sympathy for those in these stages of life, namely the old and children, yet it is right that the authority of the Rule also should have regard to them. Their weaknesses should at all times be taken into consideration, and the letter of the Rule should by no means be applied to them in matters of food. Indeed they should always be thought of compassionately, and they should have their meals before the prescribed times.

Old Men and Children

The house of God is not just a collection of ascetics, seeking a higher life by means of austerity and long prayers. It is a human family containing persons of diverse ages, from the old who have had the days of their strength, down through the years of manhood to mere children. They are seen as human beings, and so this chapter warns against a 'spiritual life' that is detached from human understanding, and insensitive to the care of the weak.

St Benedict is too wise to lay down detailed instructions; he indicates a principle: *They should always be thought of compassionately*. And the Rule itself must embody this principle. It is further illustrated in Ch. XXXI and LXX.

Chapter XXXVIII The weekly Reader

At the meals of the brethren there should always be reading, but not by anyone who happens to take up the book. There shall be a reader for the whole week, and he is to begin on Sunday. Let him begin after Mass and Communion by asking the prayers of all that God may keep from him the spirit of vanity. The reader himself is to intone the verse: *O Lord open my lips, and my mouth shall proclaim your praise*,[1] and it is to be said three times by all. And so, having received a blessing, let him begin to read. There is to be complete silence, so that no whisper nor any voice other than that of the reader be heard there. Whatever is wanted for eating and drinking the brethren should pass to one another, so that no one need ask for anything. If, however, something is wanted, it should be asked for by some sign or sound rather than by speaking. No one there present is to ask any question about the reading or about anything, so that no opportunity for disturbance may arise; unless perhaps the superior wishes to say a few words for edification. The weekly reader may take some refreshment before he begins to read because of his Holy Communion and lest his fast should be a burden to him. He is to take his meal afterwards with the weekly cooks and servers.

Mar. 17
July 17
Nov. 16

The brethren are not to read (or sing) in their order of seniority but only those who edify the listeners.

Reading at Meals

The Rule now passes to a section regulating matters connected with

[1] Ps 50:17

the refectory. The content of this chapter is double: the reader, and those who listen to him. It is eminently practical, so much so that its instructions are followed centuries after it was written.

1 Like the servers, the reader enters on his office with a prayer in which the brethren join. Like the servers of Ch. XXXV, he is rendering the brethren a service. But the prayer has a different motive. Not all were able to read in those days, and standards of public reading were high. A good reader had then some cause for complacency in his talent, his voice and his skill. Even today the advantages of education still show in a man's reading, though to read well is no longer an outstanding performance. So the object of the prayer is that he may avoid elation and vanity. Once again the never-forgotten motif of humility asserts itself.

2 As for the hearers, on them is laid the rule of *complete silence*. This is not the *taciturnitas* of Ch. VI, but a total suppression of speech and avoidance of any kind of noise. The superior may indeed say a few words but is not much encouraged to do so. The elimination of speech at meals may be found a restriction at first but, with the passage of years, it is found to be a great gain, especially when profitable reading is chosen.

3 *Because of his Holy Communion:* The brethren went to their meal after their Holy Communion. The reader who had also communicated was instructed to take a drink before beginning. One reason for this was a fear that he might perhaps spit in the course of reading.

Chapter XXXIX The Measure of Food

We consider it to be enough for the daily meal, whether at the sixth or the ninth hour, that there should always be served two cooked dishes, to allow for the weaknesses of different eaters; so that if someone cannot eat of the one dish he may still make a meal from the other. So two cooked dishes should be enough for all the brethren. And if fruit or tender vegetables are to be had, a third dish may be added. A full pound of bread should be enough for a day, whether there is one meal or those of dinner and supper. If there is a supper a third of the pound of bread should be kept back by the cellarer and produced at that meal.

Mar. 18
July 18
Nov. 17

If, however, their work is rather heavy, it will be in the Abbot's power and in his judgement to decide whether it is expedient to increase the allowance. But there must be no danger of over-eating, so that no monk is overtaken by indigestion, for there is nothing so opposed to Christian life as over-eating, as our Lord says, 'Take care that your hearts are not weighed down by over-eating.'[1] Young boys should not be given the same amount of food, but less than their elders. Frugality should be the rule on all occasions. All must refrain entirely from eating the flesh of quadrupeds, except for the sick who are really weak.

---

[1] Lk 21:34

Chapter XL The Measure of Drink

Mar. 19 July 19 Nov. 18 'Each man has his special gift from God, one of one kind, another of another kind,' [1] and hence it is with some diffidence that we fix the quantity of the food and drink of others. But keeping in view the frailty of the weak, we think that a half a pint of wine daily is enough for each. Those, however, to whom God grants the capacity to abstain should know that they will have their own reward.

If however local conditions or their work or the summer heat call for more, it must be for the superior to decide, but he must take care that neither excess nor drunkenness overtakes them. For although we read that wine is not at all a drink for monks, yet, since in our days it is impossible to persuade monks of this, let us agree at least about this that we should not drink our fill, but more sparingly, since 'wine leads even wise men into infidelity.' [2]

When however local conditions bring it about that the above mentioned quantity is not available, but much less, or none at all, then those who live there should bless God and not grumble. We lay special stress on this that the brethren remain free from grumbling.

The Measure of Food and Drink

1 Of the measure of food and drink not much need be said. Whereas St Benedict was severe and unyielding over the question of private ownership, in these matters he is accommodating, almost

[1] I Co 7:7 [2] Sir 19:2

hesitant. Of food he says modestly *We consider it to be enough . . .* and of wine *it is with some diffidence that we fix . . .* For he remains aware, as always, that in physical matters we differ widely; he is aware, too, that work or climate makes a difference.

But since food and drink are matters of self-indulgence, he considers also that they should come under the Rule. His essential requirements are few. Provision should be reasonable, but at all times heavy eating and drinking are condemned; while over-eating is contrary to Christian life altogether, and the Divine Voice warns us of the dangers of wine.

Today monks live spread out over five continents and our diet, fifteen centuries after St Benedict, is inevitably based on quite different norms from those of his century. The pages of history show us how the caricature of a monk as a heavy eater has arisen, and that these chapters were not written without good reason. Today we have an additional reason for practising frugality. Now that the world is a global village we have to bear ever in mind the condition of the under-nourished brothers of Christ wherever they may be.

2 The opening words of Ch. XL, *Each man has his special gift from God*, refer in the context specifically to abstinence, but they are capable of—and indeed have—a wider meaning. The Rule offers a basis on which those spiritual gifts which God is always ready to bestow on those who desire them, may be developed. It is not intended to impose a mediocre uniformity, but to ensure the basis of humility and self-discipline necessary so that God may give rich gifts in diversity to each of the brethren.

3 The measure of wine indicated in the Rule was a *hemina*. According to the Oxford Dictionary this was a measure of about half a pint. The point is not of great importance to us but it was, to be sure, a matter of great interest to St Benedict's first readers. 'And if ', says the Rule, 'you can't get this approved measure, *bless God and do not grumble*.' If you do the one, you are infallibly saved from the other. It is a useful tip in any matter in which short commons are involved. Indeed it is more: for to have learnt to bless, praise and thank God from the heart in adverse circumstances, be they important or trivial, is a big step towards spiritual joy.

Grumbling is referred to and condemned in no less than seven chapters. Why is so much stress laid on this point? Because St Benedict teaches that all actions are judged by God according to their dispositions. Any action done with grumbling proceeds from a faulty disposition, is sin-infected (cf. Ch. V). And further, the grumbler spreads the infection around him, lowering the general level of joyful giving to God and good will to men.

Chapter XLI At what Hours they should take their Meals

From the holy feast of Easter until Pentecost the brethren are to have their dinner at midday, and their supper in the evening. From Pentecost throughout the summer, unless the monks have work in the fields or the summer is oppressively hot, they should fast on Wednesdays and Fridays until the ninth hour, and on the other days have dinner at midday; but the midday meal may be kept up continuously throughout the week, if they have work in the fields or the summer heat is excessive; it will be for the Abbot to decide. For he is to modify and organise all their affairs in such wise that their souls may be saved, and that the brethren do whatever they do, without justification for grumbling. Mar. 20 July 20 Nov. 19

From 14 September, however, until the beginning of Lent they should always have their meal at the ninth hour.

During Lent until Easter it should be in the evening.

Vespers, however, should be sung at such an hour that the brethren will not need lamp-light for their meal, but that everything will be finished by daylight. Indeed at all seasons, the hour of supper or of the evening meal should be calculated so that everything may be done by daylight.

The Times of Meals

The Rule divided the year into three periods as far as meals were concerned: Winter, Lent, Summer—weaving the rhythm of nature into one pattern with liturgical motifs. The hours of work and prayer (and meal times too) depended far more than they do today on light and darkness, on winter and summer. In our century man dominates nature, and has to submit much less to her alternations. Moreover, monks are found today in all five continents.

Consequently the programme laid down here has lost its significance. The overall principle remains that the Abbot has to organise the work and the meals so that souls may be saved and grumbling be avoided. And this principle is well illustrated by the concession of an earlier meal to the brethren when they have to work through the longer summer hours; this is conceded by the Rule on four days in the week, the other two are left to the discretion of the Abbot.

Note: *From 14 September*: literally 'from the Ides of September' which is the 13th. But as indicated in Ch. XLVIII the change to the winter timetable was made on the 14th.

Chapter XLII That no one may speak after Compline

At all times monks ought to strive to keep silence but particularly so during the hours of the night, and this means in all seasons, whether on days of fasting or on days of having a midday meal. Mar. 21 July 21 Nov. 20

If it is the latter season, then after rising from supper, they should at once sit together and one of them should read the *Conferences* or the *Lives of the Fathers* or some other work which will edify the hearers, but not the Heptateuch or the Books of Kings; for this part of Scripture will not be helpful to those of weaker intelligence at this hour: they should, however, be read at some other time.

If it has been a fast day, then after Vespers there will be a short interval, and then they should assemble for the reading of the *Conferences* as we have said. Four or five pages should be read, or as many as the time permits; and during this space of time for reading all come together, including any one who may have been occupied in a job assigned to him.

So when all are assembled, they should say Compline, and when they come out of Compline there should be no further permission for anyone to talk about anything. If anyone is found transgressing this rule of silence he is to be punished severely, unless the need to attend to guests has arisen, or it happens that the Abbot has given someone an order. And in this case, too, the matter is to be handled with all seriousness and genuine moderation.

Spiritual Reading, Compline, Night Silence

1 After announcing the principle of the night silence, the Rule outlines the evening programme: Vespers, supper (if there had been dinner at midday), interval, reading together, enabling all to collect into one place, Compline or night prayer. There is no suggestion of the community moving to the choir for Compline; the rite is simple, uniform and known by heart. It sounds rather informal.

2 While the night silence is a matter of rule, and therefore an observance, it may well be that St Benedict thought of it almost as a doctrine: God meant the night to be a time of rest when creation gave up its activities and hushed its voice. So the night silence was a co-operation with God's plan. All the Rule is imbued with the thought of returning to God by obedience and co-operation with God's creative plan. If then we think of the night as the time when God says to his creation: Be quiet now, sleep and take your rest, there is a certain rightness in our accepting it as a time of deeper silence. Such silence, being allied to the divine order, has about it a certain sacredness.

3 Characteristically the chapter ends with a reference to possible exceptions—pilgrims would be likely to travel all day and look for a monastery as night fell. The Abbot then may dispense with silence but only as much as each case demands.

4 The *Heptateuch*: this was the Pentateuch with Joshua and Judges. By *weaker intelligence* St Benedict seems to mean 'over-lively imagination'.

The uniting thought that runs through the group of Chapters XLIII–XLVI is that of incomplete observance. As there is tepidity in prayer, so there is slackness of observance. In both cases the result is loss, more or less great, and in various ways these chapters seek to forestall this.

Chapter XLIII Latecomers to the Work of God or to Meals

As soon as the signal for the Divine Office is heard, the brethren must leave whatever they have been engaged in doing, and hasten with all speed; but with dignity, so that foolishness finds no stimulus. Nothing, therefore, is to be given preference over the Work of God. Mar. 22 July 22 Nov. 21

If at the Night Office anyone arrives after the *Glory be* of Psalm 94, which for this reason we wish to be said altogether slowly and deliberately, he must not stand in his place in the choir, but last of all, or in a place set apart by the Abbot for such careless persons, so that they may be seen by the Abbot and by everyone else, until at the end of the Work of God he does penance by public satisfaction. We have thought it best that such persons should stand last or else apart, so that being shamed because they are noticed by everybody, they may for this motive mend their ways. For if they stay outside the oratory, there may be someone who will go back and go to sleep again, or maybe sit down outside the oratory and give himself up to gossip, and in this way an opportunity is given to the evil one; it is better that they go in and not lose the benefit of the whole Office: and they should mend their ways as well.

At the Day Hours anyone who has not arrived at the Work of God after the versicle and the *Glory be* of the first Psalm that follows it, must take the last place as we have laid down above, nor may he take for granted permission to join the choir as they sing, until he has made satisfaction, unless the Abbot pardons him and gives him permission; nevertheless one guilty of this fault should still make satisfaction.

Mar. 23 July 23 Nov. 22 With regard to meals, the brother who does not arrive before the verse, so that all may say the verse and pray together and go to their meal together, that is the brother who does not arrive either through carelessness or other fault, should be admonished twice for this behaviour. If then he does not amend, he will not be permitted to share the common meal, but will be separated from the companionship of the others to eat alone, and will be deprived of his portion of wine, until he makes satisfaction and improves. The same applies to any one who absents himself from the verse said after the meal.

Moreover, no one should be so bold as to take any food or drink before or after the regular meal time. But if something is offered to a brother by the superior and he rejects it, then when he does want what he previously rejected, or something else, he is not to receive anything at all until he makes suitable satisfaction.

Penances for Unpunctuality

1 St Benedict teaches that the brethren should think of none of their works as more important than the Work of God. Hence when the bell goes one must hastily disengage oneself for the more important task. What task can be more important than our audience with God? Intrinsically, none; even if at times charity or necessity requires exceptions or modifies the situation.

2 But one may be late, not because one has failed to stop work, but because one has failed to get out of bed. One reaches the door, to find, like the unwise bridesmaids, that it is shut, and will not be opened. Now what to do? Sleep? Sit down? Have a chat? But the prayer, thinks St Benedict, is too valuable for that—one is reminded of the enthusiasms of modern charismatics who arrive at their prayer-meetings with a vivid consciousness of something to be gained. Hence the decision: let the latecomers go in, and not lose the whole of it, and do better next time. But he makes the condition that, subject to the Abbot's judgement, they should suffer a certain penalty. So they must stand apart and wait for permission to join in.

3 Something similar is laid down for meals, but in this case the remedy for unpunctuality is more obvious. He who is late through negligence takes his meal later, and loses his portion of wine as well. Likewise he who, having done his own eating, departs, is considered an offender.

What exactly is at stake? It is not merely a matter of punctuality and good order that lies behind these regulations. The common meal was a social and religious activity beginning with the praise of God, provider of all good things, served fraternally, consumed by the fraternity as such, and concluded by their prayer of thanksgiving. It involved rather more than the silent filling of a human body, for notwithstanding the strict silence and the simplicity of what was served, it was a communal celebration. And for this reason the respect implied in arriving in time and staying till the end was due to it. And the notion of excommunication could be applied to it.

4 Why has a brother done wrong if he refuses what the superior offered him? Presumably the superior's offer was prompted, not by a desire to favour or pamper, but by a judgement on his need. It was an act of compassion. 'You had better stop fasting and take a snack before the regular meal time.' This called for a humble acceptance, and the refusal was a mark of pride.

Chapter XLIV How the Excommunicated are to make Satisfaction

Mar. 24
July 24
Nov. 23

If, for serious faults, anyone is excommunicated from the oratory and from the common meals, he is to lie prostrate at the threshold of the oratory at the time when the Work of God is being carried out, saying nothing, but just lying there with his head to the ground at the feet of them all as they come out of the oratory. This he is to continue to do until the Abbot considers the satisfaction to be enough. When at the Abbot's bidding he comes in, he must cast himself at the feet of the Abbot and then at the feet of the others, that they may pray for him. Then following the Abbot's instructions he may be admitted into Choir or in such position as the Abbot decides, but on condition that he does not presume to sing alone any Psalm or reading or anything else, until the Abbot gives a fresh order. Moreover, at every hour, when the Work of God is being finished, he is to cast himself on the ground in the place where he is standing. And so must continue to do penance, until the Abbot again orders him to stop making this satisfaction.

With regard to those who for less serious faults are excommunicated from meals only, they are to make satisfaction in the oratory until the Abbot orders them to stop. They perform this penance until the Abbot gives his blessing and says, 'That is enough.'

Procedure for the Excommunicated

1 The theme dealt with here might have been treated in Ch. XXIII

– XXX. The difference is that those chapters treat the matter from the point of view of the sentence to be imposed; here it is treated in terms of an observance—what the culprit should and should not do.

2 It is to be noticed that even in the case of the graver excommunication a link is kept between the excommunicated brother and the community. Cut off he may be; forgotten he cannot be; so he is instructed to pray silently but visibly for the prayers of the brethren.

3 Everything in this chapter speaks of the methods of a long past age. Has it any significance for us today? These sanctions for defects are really the obverse of the medal. Behind them we discern the strong sense of community life—they belong to a society which sees itself as a closely knit family of God, whose standards are high, and for all its ascetic prescriptions has no doubt about offering 'good days' (cf. Prologue) to its members. Its worst threat is to say to an impenitent member: Henceforth you belong to us no more.

Chapter XLV Those who make Mistakes in the Oratory

Mar. 25 July 25 Nov. 24 If anyone goes wrong in giving out a Psalm, responsory, antiphon or reading, unless by making satisfaction he humbles himself there before all, he must submit to greater punishment; for he refused to put right with humility what he did wrong through lack of care. And boys should be beaten for such a fault.

Satisfaction for Mistakes at the Divine Office

The fact of having to make satisfaction for mistakes that disturb the course of the Divine Office is seen as the cure for negligence, and maybe also for distraction, and it is enforced by warning of a heavier penalty.

If this seems to us somewhat strenuous, it is much milder than we might encounter in a training course of Zen meditation.

It is important to grasp that the object is not an unkind one, nor to force a person to pray against their will, but to aid him to pray as his will wants, and to secure the best conditions for all. In fact one who gives a wrong Psalm or antiphon does mar the prayer of all.

Chapter XLVI Those who commit Faults in other Matters

If any one while engaged in his work, in the kitchen, in the cellarer's offices, in the storeroom, in the bakery, in the garden or while engaged in any craft, or indeed anywhere else, behaves badly or breaks some article or destroys it, or commits some excess, he should come straightaway before the Abbot and the community, declare his transgression and make satisfaction. But if he does not do this, and the transgression becomes known through another, he must undergo a heavier penalty.

Mar. 26
July 26
Nov. 25

However, if the failing be an interior sin, he should declare it only to the Abbot, or to spiritual fathers, for they, knowing how to heal their own wounds, know how to heal those of others, without revealing them or making them known.

Satisfaction for other Faults

1 There is more to common life than non-ownership of personal property. The value and power of common prayer is another aspect, and one which the Rule surrounds with safeguards (Ch. XLIII and XLV). Behind this chapter lies the assumption that the work of the brethren is also a common effort, whether performed in a group or not. It is a treasury of merit to which all contribute. It is not indeed expected that all should contribute perfectly—that would be superhuman. But when someone has failed the community or damaged its peaceful life through a wrong action (for example, bad temper, bad language) or damaged its temporal assets (not easily replaceable in those days) he owes it to all to admit his fault. To do wrong or break things is human; to say nothing about it is anti-social as if one were responsible only to oneself. Moreover, to understand how this legislation would be profitable one has to grasp two things. First, the individual monk is presumed to be seeking to advance always in humility, the basis of progress towards God. Second, the community is united in love, and that makes the confession of misdemeanour a matter of sympathy and edification.

2 Very significant are the last words. The spiritual fathers are considered to have learnt how to heal spiritual wounds. Many of our sins are latent or proceed from latent causes, best described as wounds or traumata. Now one may absolve sins, but the wounds of the soul call for healing or, as we call it, inner healing.

These wounds are of two kinds: in the moral order are vices, besetting temptations, sinful thoughts; on the psychological level there are such sufferings as are caused by depressions, deep-set grievances, sense of alienation, etc.

3 The inwardness of this chapter may be appreciated by comparing it with Bonhoeffer's thought:

> Despite sharing in worship, praying together and despite all communal service, Christians often remain isolated; the final breakthrough to real fellowship is not achieved, because they form a fellowship as believers, as devout Christians, but not as irreligious people, as sinners. Consequently each must conceal his sins from himself and from the community. . .
>
> It is in confession that the breakthrough occurs. Sin seeks to be alone with the person involved, it draws him away from the community. . .
>
> In confession the light of the Gospel breaks into the darkness and stubbornness of the heart.[1]

So far St Benedict has set out his main doctrines on the monastic life, and the structure by which the house is held together; he has had much to say about the prayer-life of the monk, of his sleep and sleeping quarters, of the cellarer's department, and matters connected with the refectory, and of penitential satisfaction. In the next somewhat miscellaneous section, his eye ranges round the monastery and its premises, and answers some questions about relations with the outside world (Ch. XLVII–LVII).

---

[1] Quoted by H. Mühlen, *A Charismatic Theology*, Burns and Oates, 1978, p.86

Chapter XLVII The Signal for the Work of God

To give the signal for the Work of God, whether by day or by night, is the responsibility of the Abbot. He may do it himself or he may lay the charge on a brother sufficiently responsible to ensure that everything is performed at the correct time. The intoning of Psalms and antiphons is to be done in turn after the Abbot by those appointed. No one should venture to sing or read unless he can do it to the edification of his hearers. It is to be done with humility, gravity and reverence, and by appointment of the Abbot.

Mar. 27
July 27
Nov. 26

Official Tasks at the Divine Office

1 The Rule leaves to common sense the question of how to inform the brethren of the next item on the programme. But to summon the brethren to the Work of God is a different matter, being a reminder that now is the time for God's hour and an invitation to his presence. It was then a task of religious significance and is made the direct responsibility of the Abbot. It is not below his dignity to perform this task himself, though he may delegate it.

2 The reference to the selection of monks for different parts in the Divine Office is not just a sign of an organising mentality. The point stressed is that all may be done in the way that gives God the most worship: *with humility*, *gravity* and *reverence*, that is, with the realisation of the seriousness of what one is doing.

Chapter XLVIII The daily manual Labour

Mar. 28 July 28 Nov. 27 Idleness is the enemy of the soul. For this reason the brethren should be occupied at certain times in manual labour, and at other times in sacred reading. Hence we think that the times for these two duties may be arranged as follows:

From Easter till 14 September, they should set out in the morning and work at whatever is necessary from the first hour till about the fourth. From the fourth hour till about the sixth, they should be engaged in reading. After the sixth hour, and when they have had their meal, they may rest on their beds in complete silence, or if anyone has a mind to read, he may do so, but in such a way as not to disturb anyone else. None should be said rather early, at about the middle of the eighth hour, and then they should work again at whatever their tasks are until Vespers. If, however, local necessity or their own poverty compels them to work personally at gathering the harvest, they should not be upset about this. For then truly are they monks, if they live by the work of their hands, as did our Fathers and the Apostles. All their labours, however, should be kept under control on account of the less courageous.

Mar. 29 July 29 Nov. 28 From 14 September until the beginning of Lent they should be free for reading till the end of the second hour. Then Terce should be said, and all should work at their allotted tasks until None. At the first signal for None every brother should detach himself from his work, so as to be ready for the sounding of the second signal. After their evening meal they should give themselves to reading or to studying the Psalms.

In Lent, however, the hours for reading are from the morning until the end of the third hour. Then until the end of the tenth hour they should work at their allotted tasks. And during these days of Lent everyone should receive a book from the library, which he should read through from the beginning. These books are to be given out at the beginning of Lent. It is important that one or two seniors should be appointed to go round the monastery during the hours when the brethren are engaged in reading, to see whether perchance they come upon some lazy brother who is engaged in doing nothing or in chatter, and is not intent upon his book, and so not only profitless to himself but leading others astray. If such a one is found (which we hope will not be the case) he should be reprimanded once and a second time and if he does not amend, he should be punished in accordance with the Rule, so that the others may be warned.

Moreover a brother should not be in the company of another at the wrong time.

On Sunday all should give themselves to reading, Mar. 30 July 30 Nov. 29
except those to whom other duties have been assigned. But if anyone is so careless and idle that he is either unwilling or unable to study or read, he must be given some other task so as not to be unemployed.

To the brethren who are in poor health or not strong, the work or craft that is allotted should be such as to keep them occupied, but not such as by its weight to break them down or drive them away. Their lack of strength is a matter for the Abbot's consideration.

The Hours of Work and of spiritual Reading

1 What was St Benedict's attitude towards work? The principle *idleness is the enemy of the soul* is rather negative. It shows only an aim to promote a balanced life such as would accord with the good spiritual condition of the monks. He takes it for granted that his monks will have to work for their living, and even finds advantage rather than loss in the situation mentioned later in which the brethren will have to work harder than is convenient under the sheer compulsion of getting a living. And he expects the monastery to have the assistance of craftsmen. Crafts demand skill and concentration. When in later ages monks became priests and were better educated than other men, their work acquired significance for a wider world. It was no longer to be described as merely 'a work of the hands' but was intellectual, scientific, educational, apostolic, missionary. The seeds of all this are found in the Rule itself and illustrated further in St Gregory's life of St Benedict. Once developed neither these values nor the problems acquired with them would ever be lost again. The monastic life became richer in its fulfilment of human personality and in its usefulness to society, but at the cost of its primeval simplicity. Many a monastery would be founded in order to recover that gift.

The monks then came to understand that their Rule had a germinal quality, and to accept the pluralism which it gave rise to. For the monk was trained by his Rule not to be an isolated ascetic, but a well-balanced Christian and a member of a small Christian society; and that small society did not turn its back on the needs of other Christians, and of Christian society as a whole. Both the negative and the positive aspects of this chapter would lay the basis of a vast development, in which monks adapted to the needs and circumstances of the most varied times and places.

2 The situation is mentioned in which the monks, owing to *local necessity or their own poverty*, have to join in the harvesting themselves. This seems to imply that, their own property being inadequate, they have to hire themselves out to work for other men. This makes them comparable *to our Fathers and the Apostles*, who gained their living without benefit of landed property of their own. No doubt this kind of work on the harvest combined with the Night Office meant a tough programme; and the warning that the Abbot was to keep the situation *under control on account of the less courageous* was realistic enough.

3 Sacred reading (*lectio divina*) is mentioned as an element in the day's programme. Indeed it was a constitutive element in the monastic programme. It corresponds more or less to what we call spiritual reading, but with a distinct emphasis of its own; it supposes that the reader's ears are attuned to the divine message as he reads. He is not reading for entertainment, nor scientific study, nor to prepare a sermon, but in all simplicity that he may learn more of divine things. This may be difficult for us moderns, since our education is such as to make us critical evaluators of what we read. Nor is this in itself a false attitude, but it is a different one. Such reading will not be the gateway to prayer that is presumed in this chapter.

Chapter XLIX The Observance of Lent

Mar. 31 July 31 Nov. 30 Although the monk's life ought at all seasons to bear a Lenten character such strength is found only in the few. Therefore we urge the brethren to keep the days of Lent with a special purity of life and also at this holy season to make reparation for the failings of other times. This reparation will be worthily performed if we guard ourselves from all our faults and apply ourselves to prayer with tears, to reading, to compunction of heart and to abstinence. Therefore at this season let us increase in some way the normal standard of our service, as for example, by special prayers, or by a diminution in food and drink; and so let each one spontaneously in the joy of the Holy Spirit[1] make some offering to God concerning the allowance granted him. Thus he may reduce food and drink for his body, or his sleep, or his talkativeness or his looseness in speech, and so with the joy of spiritual desire, look forward to holy Easter.

But every brother should propose to the Abbot whatever he intends to offer, and it should be performed with his blessing and approval. For anything done without the permission of the spiritual father will be put down to presumption and vainglory, and deserving no reward. Everything, therefore, must be carried out with the approval of the Abbot.

How to make the most of Lent

1 *Such strength is found only in the few:* Abbot Poemon (dc 450) said;

[1] cf. Rm 14:17

'I used to live in spirit with Holy Mary, Mother of God, weeping beside the Cross of the Saviour, and I wished so to weep always.' This was the authentic voice of early monasticism. But it is indeed a special vocation requiring a deep identification with the Paschal Mystery that fits a man to live in this way. Lent, then, is a special period in which the monk seeks to grow in the understanding of this Mystery which is at the very heart of the Christian understanding of life—and therefore of the monastic vocation.

And what exactly is this Paschal Mystery? It is this fact that Christ overcame the world and the kingdom of darkness by his death on the Cross. In the total sacrifice of himself he manifested the depth of God's love for us sinners. His death was his victory. In the Resurrection the Father manifested his own acceptance of the human race in the person of his Son, whom he raised in triumph to be Lord and Saviour of the world. In Christ we are 'incorporated', joined, that is, to him by an invisible bond of grace and sharing all that is his—his Spirit, his glory, his triumph over evil.

That is why the brother is bidden to prepare for the Easter feast *with the joy of spiritual desire.* References to spiritual joy in the Rule usually occur in connection with some sacrifice to be made (cf. end of Prologue and the fourth degree of humility). Here significantly joy is mentioned as the concomitant of the acts of individual self-denial to which the brother is invited, and as the concomitant of the unfulfilled longing for the greater joy that is the special gift of the Easter feast. We have to learn that the joy and peace of Christ radiate from the Holy Pasch, and that the feast casts its light beforehand on him who prepares and remains afterwards as a residing grace.

2 An aspect of Lent mentioned, not here, but in the preceding chapter is that of additional sacred reading. Lent was to be also a season of increased learning about the spiritual life. It was not a sad season, but one rich in spiritual progress for those who would make the effort.

3 *Prayer with tears* and *compunction of heart*: these gifts of God's Spirit are a favourite motif. Cf. Ch. IV, XX and LII.

Chapter L Brethren who work far from the Oratory, or who are on a Journey

Apr. 1 Aug. 1 Dec. 1

Brethren whose work is at a considerable distance, and who cannot reach the oratory at the right time—and the Abbot recognises this to be the case—should perform the Work of God in the place where they are working, kneeling down in deep respect to God. And likewise those who are travelling should not allow the hours prescribed for prayer to go unobserved, but they should do their best to carry out their duties in God's service and not neglect them.

Inability to attend the Divine Office

The directives concern those who for any reason cannot be present at the Divine Office. In spite of the maxim 'Let nothing be preferred to the Work of God' such things occur. But, then says St Benedict, let them praise God, with due reverence, where they are, and as far as possible at the appropriate times. In the last analysis, the Work of God is not something identified with church worship; it is rooted in the brother's sense of his *duties in God's service*, a loving duty indeed but one that always urges.

Chapter LI Brethren who go out on short Errands

If a brother is sent out on some errand, and expects to return to the monastery the same day, he must not assume permission to eat outside the monastery, even if the invitation is a very pressing one, unless he has been so instructed by the Abbot. Anyone who does otherwise is to be excommunicated.

Apr. 2
Aug. 2
Dec. 2

Permission to eat outside the Monastery

1 The words *on some errand* do not necessarily refer to business such as buying and selling. They would surely include the exercise of the corporal works of mercy listed in Ch. IV (to relieve the poor, etc.). There were also the spiritual works of mercy, such as instructing the ignorant in the faith. We know that St Benedict did this himself both at Subiaco and at Monte Cassino (cf. *Dialogues II* 1,2,4,8).

2 The laity are hospitable, and like to invite the monks to take refreshment. This could lead to abuse. St Benedict does not absolutely forbid accepting such kindness, but lays down that the Abbot must be asked for permission first. The latter may well consider whether it is a one-meal or a two-meal day, the length and frequency of the expedition, whether hardship will be inflicted, etc. But the monk does well to ask himself first whether what he wants is good and praiseworthy; so that the Abbot's approval becomes his normal response.

Chapter LII The Oratory of the Monastery

Apr. 3 Aug. 3 Dec. 3 The oratory should correspond to its name, and not be used for any other purpose, nor to store things. When the Work of God has been completed all are to go out noiselessly, and let reverence for God reign there. So that if a brother should have a mind to pray by himself, he will not be disturbed by the ill-conduct of anyone else. Moreover, also on other occasions, if someone wishes to make a private prayer, let him go in without hesitation and pray, not however aloud, but with tears, and the attention of his heart. Anyone therefore, who is not engaged on such a task, is not allowed to remain in the oratory after the Work of God, as we said above, lest someone else be disturbed.

The Use of the Oratory

1 The monastery of St Benedict's day has not yet learned to call itself an Abbey, nor yet to build an Abbey Church; all that will come when monasteries develop into centres of pilgrimage. At this stage the oratory or place of prayer is a very simple place, and the Rule thinks it necessary to lay down that it is not to be used for doing or keeping anything else. (The Egyptian monks had the custom of combining prayer with a simple form of work such as mat-making.)

2 The brother who wishes to pray personally must do so silently and not aloud—and this for the sake of others. In antiquity, less bound by rigid conventions than ourselves, to pray aloud spontaneously was common enough. When the priest Eli saw Anna praying silently and could not hear her, he concluded she was drunk.[1]

3 The large open-handed gesture '*let him go in without hesitation*',

[1] Is 1:12,13

no questions asked, is noteworthy. The freedom given here is freedom to fulfil desire and reap the fruits of God's giving.

4 Noteworthy, too, are the words *with tears and the attention of his heart*. These are not tears of sadness, but of compunction, a joyful quality resulting from the simultaneous pressures of the sense of one's own unworthiness and the overwhelming goodness of God. *Attention of heart*: that is to say with the heart homing in on God.

Chapter LIII The Reception of Guests

Apr. 4 Aug. 4 Dec. 4 All who arrive as guests are to be welcomed like Christ, for he is going to say, 'I was a stranger and you welcomed me.'[1] The respect due to their station is to be shown to all, particularly to those of one family with us in the faith[2] and to pilgrims. As soon as a guest is announced he should be met by the superior or by brethren with every expression of charity, and first of all they should pray together, and then greet one another with the kiss of peace. This kiss of peace should not be offered until after prayer has been said, since the devil sometimes plays tricks. When guests arrive or depart the greatest humility should be shown in addressing them: so, let Christ who is received in them be adored with bowed head or prostrate body.

So when the guests have been welcomed they should be led to prayer, and then either the superior or some one delegated by him should sit with them. The Divine Law should be read to them for their edification, and after this every kindness should be shown to them. The superior may break the fast for the sake of a guest unless it happens to be an important fast day which cannot be waived; the brethren, however, should keep their accustomed fasts.

The Abbot should give all the guests water to wash their hands, and with the whole community he should wash their feet. When they have done so, they should recite the verse: *We have received your mercy, O God, in the midst of your temple.*[3]

---

[1] Mt 25:35 [2] cf. Ga 6:10 [3] Ps 47:10

Special care is to be shown in the reception of the poor and of pilgrims, for in them especially is Christ received; for the awe felt for the wealthy imposes respect enough of itself.

The kitchen for the Abbot and guests should be separate, so that when guests arrive at unforeseeable times (and they are always coming to a monastery) they may not disturb the brethren. Two brethren capable of performing this duty should take over this kitchen for a year. Help should be given them as they need it, so that they may serve without complaint, and also, when they have less work to do, they should leave their kitchen to work wherever they are bidden. And this principle applies not only to them but to all departments of the monastery: help is to be provided for those in need, and when they have spare time, they must obey their orders. Apr. 5 Aug. 5 Dec. 5

Also, with regard to the guests' quarters, a brother should be put in charge, whose soul is filled with the fear of God. A sufficient number of beds should be kept ready there. And let God's house be wisely cared for by wise men.

No one without specific instructions is to associate or converse with the guests. If a brother should meet one or see one, he should, as we have said, give him a humble greeting, and then ask a blessing and go on his way, explaining that he is not allowed to converse with a guest.

Reception and Care of Guests

1 Three items are treated: (1) the principles that concern the reception of guests, somewhat mixed with (2) the ritual employed for receiving special guests; and then (3) the practical dispositions that are necessary so that the guests do not disturb the rhythm and way of life of the brethren. The tradition of receiving every Christian as a brother came from the earliest ages of the Church, when the door of every Christian was open to the traveller. It was an aspect of early church life kept alive by the monasteries.

It is clear that guests can be of various kinds. There are the important and highly placed ones to be received with suitable honour; there are the poorer sort to be received with less pomp but more tenderness, because in them Christ is recognised more clearly; and there are ordinary guests, too—but always there is somebody. They may even be the wrong kind. Credentials may want looking into before some people are received; this is done by reading the Gospel to them.

The essential principle is that Christ is received in every guest. Hence he is not received with condescension but with humility and charity. The community does not look down on its guests from the pinnacle of its spiritual life or the grandeur of its establishment; it thinks in terms of Christ's words in the Gospel.

But what of the strange person who disappears the moment it is proposed to read the Gospel to him? The reference is to a possible visit from the devil himself. It sounds very unsophisticated and credulous to us. Yet in our times, after the complacent materialism of the last century, we are becoming much more aware of diabolic influence in our society. Satanists and addicts to evil powers are to be found at work; and there are persons over whom evil powers have established some kind of control or influence. Phenomena in which evil power plays a part are not so rare today.

2 *Every kindness (*humanitas*) should be shown him:* A golden sentence. For in this way the traveller recognises most easily that he is among the disciples of Christ, and, if he is burdened with spiritual troubles, will be encouraged to ask for help about them.

3 Guests *are always coming to a monastery:* A whole apostolate is indicated in a few words. 'The preoccupation with the neighbour', writes Fr Jean LeClerq, 'is certainly a salient characteristic of contemporary spirituality.' There are different ways of meeting this challenge. Does not a whole legion of lost souls or badly worn ones await the attention of monasteries in which they can recognise a society not founded on go-getting? It is the kind of apostolate in which Benedictine traditions and modern needs seem to find a common focus.

4 *And let God's house be wisely cared for:* In this context the words refer to practical arrangements rather than to spiritual ones. It is characteristic of the spirituality of the Rule not to neglect this aspect of life, but to honour God also in the care of his created things, and to build the spiritual house in a well-ordered material one. The words summarise perfectly the hope that lies behind the material regulations; to some extent the regulations are of a past age, but the attitude is not.

Chapter LIV Whether a Monk should receive Letters or other Gifts

Apr. 6 Aug. 6 Dec. 6 On no account may a monk, without the Abbot's permission, either accept (or give) letters or offerings of blessed bread or small gifts of any kind whether from his parents or other people or his brethren. And if something is sent to him, even from his parents, he must not take upon himself to accept it before it has been shown to the Abbot. If the Abbot allows it to be accepted, it rests with him to decide to whom it shall be given, and the brother to whom it was sent must not be upset, so that no opportunity is given the evil one. If anyone should be headstrong enough to act otherwise he must submit to the discipline of the Rule.

Letters and Small Gifts

The chapter reads rather stiffly. St Benedict is unyielding in what concerns the common life. Parents show much the same characteristics in all generations: they love us; often they think we have chosen a hard lot, and are anxious to mitigate the consequences of our folly. Nor is it only parents who do not appreciate the significance of common life. For the world at large sees it (correctly) as the denial of a very deep human instinct, but does not see it as having its roots in the fulfilment of a charity enterprising enough to build a new social order; or, more exactly, to seek to reproduce the social ideals of the apostolic age. If, as can happen, the brethren also fail to see it that way, the common life stands always to suffer diminution one way or another; or it will be maintained as a barren juridical structure, lacking charismatic *élan*.

It should be remembered, too, that gifts, even small gifts, can reflect a distinction of class. Gifts cost money or imply possessions, and parents vary in their capacity to give. It may happen that a brother has been rejected by his parents; orphans have no parents;

some brethren have a whole tribe of loving relatives . . . a little thought shows why the Rule considered it necessary to impose a control.

Chapter LV The Clothing and Footwear of the Brethren

Apr. 7 Aug. 7 Dec. 7 Clothing should be given to the brethren according to the nature of the district where they live and the climate, because in cold places more is needed and in warm ones less. This is for the Abbot to consider. It is our view that in temperate localities, it will be sufficient for monks if each has a cowl and a tunic—the cowl thick and woolly in winter, but thin or worn in summer—and a scapular for work. For footwear he should have stockings and shoes. The monks should not argue about the colour or coarseness of all these things, but accept what is available in the region where they live or can be bought cheaply.

But the Abbot should take care about the size of these clothes, that they are not too short for those who use them, but of the right size. Those who receive new clothes should always give the old ones back at once; they can be stored in the wardrobe for the benefit of the poor. For it is sufficient for a monk to have two tunics and two cowls, to allow for wear at night and for washing: more than that is superfluous, and should be taken away. Their stockings also and anything that is old should be returned by them when they get new ones.

Those who are sent on a journey should get drawers from the wardrobe, which they should wash and give back on their return. Also their cowls and tunics should be in rather better condition than those they usually have; they should get them from the wardrobe when they set out on this journey, and give them back on their return.

For bedding, a mattress, a blanket, a coverlet and a pillow are enough. The beds should be frequently inspected by the Abbot as a precaution against private possessions. If anyone is found to have anything which was not given him by the Abbot, he is to undergo the severest punishment; and that this vice of personal ownership may be totally eliminated, everything necessary should be given by the Abbot; namely, a cowl, a tunic, stockings, shoes, a belt, a knife, a pen, a needle, a handkerchief and writing tablets, so that all excuses about necessity are removed. But the Abbot must always bear in mind the statement in the Acts of the Apostles that 'distribution was made to each according to his need.'[1] And so he must bear in mind the weakness of those in need, but not the ill-will of the envious. Indeed in all his decisions he must consider that God will repay.

Apr. 8
Aug. 8
Dec. 8

Clothing, Footwear, General Equipment

1 In physical matters St Benedict is always careful to allow latitude, and here he contents himself with a general principle and his own view of what is adequate in climates that he knows.

2 *A scapular for work:* The word *scapulare* cannot be translated satisfactorily since the article no longer exists in the original sense. It was, says Dom McCann, 'an article designed to constrict the loose habit and prevent it from impeding the free use of the limbs. . . ' It involved both shoulders and arms.[2] It was put on much as a modern person might put on an apron. The modern

---

[1] Ac 4:35

[2] The Rule of St Benedict, p.192n. Burns Oates and Washbourne, 1952

monk's scapular is simply a loose, flowing outer garment—in fact something usually taken off for manual work.

3 The enactment that the Abbot must see that all garments, even if inexpensive ones, fit the wearer is one of many indications of respect for human personality found in the Rule. No doubt Christ's dress was poor, but it was not grotesque. And so also with all material needs: the brethren are not to be denied things necessary for whatever they have to do. But the principle inculcated here as in Ch. XXXIV is that of the need of the individual—not of the weight he can pull.

4 No attempt is to be made to impress the outside world with a demonstration of the asceticism practised in the cloister. When the brethren go out, they are to be provided with rather better dress than usual.

5 Among the articles for normal distribution are a pen and writing materials. If we combine this with the extensive provision for spiritual reading, we see that a certain intellectual life is anticipated, and that the expression *the work of the hands* or manual labour (Ch. XLVIII) is not to be understood too narrowly. It is true that St Benedict's attitude to culture is rather negative. However, the culture of his times has been described as 'a pseudo-culture, oratorical, imitative, founded in moribund paganism'. And, incidentally, are there not many valueless elements, stridently proclaiming themselves in our culture today?

The Rule placed in the hands of the monks such tools of culture as were available; they also had boys to teach. In time a new and vigorous culture would grow up.

Chapter LVI The Abbot's Table

The Abbot should always take his meals with the guests Apr. 9
and pilgrims. Whenever there are no guests he may at Aug. 9 Dec. 9
his own discretion invite to his table from among the brethren those whom he wishes, but one or two seniors should always be left with the brethren for the sake of discipline.

The Abbot's Table

A small chapter indeed, but pregnant with consequences, some of them unfortunate. The Abbot, as a matter of hospitality, is to take his meals with the guests and there is a special kitchen to provide the necessary service (Ch. LIII). The guests' refectory and their quarters will obviously be built closely together. And so arises the germ of the Abbot's quarters, which will grow and come in time to be called the *Abbatiatus*. It was to this part of the establishment that the ever-growing number of pilgrims made their way. For them the terminus of their journey was this *Abbatiat*. In time it gave its name to the whole complex, and so the monastery itself came to be known as *Abbatia*, or Abbey.

Centuries pass and conditions change. Pilgrims can arrange to arrive at reasonable hours. Guests' refectory and kitchen have disappeared, Abbot and brethren and guests share one meal today.

One or two seniors: the ruling is based on the assumption that the monastery has no Prior. This appointment is not discussed before Ch. LXV.

Chapter LVII The Craftsmen of the Monastery

Apr. 10 Aug. 10 Dec. 10 If there are craftsmen in the monastery let them carry on their crafts in all humility, subject to the approval of the Abbot. But if any one of them becomes conceited because of his knowledge of his craft, which is apparently bringing profit to the monastery, he is to be taken away from his craft; nor is he to come back to it, unless, after he has shown humility, the Abbot gives him a new permission. If anything produced by the craftsmen is to be sold, those responsible for the transaction must take care not to venture to do anything fraudulent. They should always keep in mind the fate of Ananias and Sapphira, lest the death which those persons incurred in the body, they (and any who practise fraud in the affairs of the monastery) should themselves undergo in their souls.

With regard to the prices charged, the sin of avarice must not creep in; but whatever is sold should be a little cheaper than is possible for lay-persons, 'so that God may be glorified in all things.'[1]

The Craftsmen

1 The pen is by no means the only instrument of culture; there are also arts and crafts alluded to several times in the Rule (cf. Ch. XLVI, XLVIII, LXVI). 'Nothing', said Péguy, 'is so civilizing as a trade that one knows well and plies with care and devotion.' It is not the object of life—for man is made for the love and worship of his Creator—yet it is something at his service, enabling him to exercise some slight shadow of God's creative power; therefore it

---

[1] I P 4:11

is a cause of joy. St Benedict encourages the craftsman for he provides that he shall normally continue to practise his skill; nor is he speaking of 'hobbies', but of crafts by which men gain their living. Unconsciously he is laying a basis for the whole resurgent culture of Europe. He is aware, however, that the very joy in craftsmanship and the success that comes with acquired skill may have their temptations. The monk is essentially God's workman, and if that character is imperilled, the craft may have to be suspended.

2 There is a second danger to be avoided—not so much for the craftsman as for those *responsible for the transaction*. Let them beware of fraud. The fraud referred to here is not precisely that of cheating the buyer but of retaining some part of the proceeds. The sin of Ananias and Sapphira lay, not in the conduct of the sale of their property, but in deceiving the Holy Spirit by saying, 'This is all' when it was not all. And so here the fundamental thought is this: Whatever a monk gains he gains for the community, just as whatever he loses (cf. Ch. XLVI) is their loss. Spiritual and material gain, spiritual and material loss, enrich or impoverish the whole body.

3 *Whatever is sold should be a little cheaper:* A monastery that did this on a considerable scale today would probably be thought of as trying to 'corner' the market! The business world would not easily be convinced that it was done that God might be glorified. And how is God glorified in this way? The monk resists the temptation to avarice. The buyer is happy with a good deal. At the lowest he will not feel that 'the Church' (as he may call the monks) has driven a hard deal with him; at the best he may even be stimulated to praise God. At any rate it is clear to him that in God's house a certain kindness accompanies honesty in human transactions.

4 Indeed, *that God may be glorified in all things* is the key to human sanctity. For sanctity implies the exploitation of every human action and situation to God's glory. It is the secret demonstrated in the lives of the saints. The point is made here because buying and selling would seem to be the part of the monk's life nearest to the pattern of the ways of the world, and correspondingly remote from the service of praise. Hence the insistence that God is to be glorified in it—not merely by a passing thought—but by the entry of kindliness and self-restraint into the deal itself. It is when God is glorified and praised and made part of all life's transactions that life becomes rich, and progress is made in sanctity. Thus also is the dualism of dividing life simply into the sacred (directed to God alone) and the profane (at best useless, maybe worse) is avoided.

In the Old Testament 'the skill and perception and knowledge for every kind of craft' was seen as a divine gift, the craftsman being 'filled with the spirit of God'.[2]

When the Son of God became incarnate he accepted our flesh and all its material surroundings. He taught us, not to reject his creation, but to use it for his honour. And when he made tables and chairs, without doubt he sold them at kindly prices.

---

[2] Ex 31:2–4

With the next chapter begins a new series of themes. They concern the reception of various kinds of newcomers, and the making of new appointments (Ch. LVIII–LXVI).

3
The Renovation of the Monastery

Chapter LVIII The Rules for receiving Brethren

Easy admission is not to be granted to anyone as soon as he applies to enter the monastic state, but as the Apostle says, 'test the Spirits to see whether they are of God.'[1] But if the newcomer continues to knock on the door, and it is seen that he puts up patiently with the unkind replies and the difficulty of getting in, and that after four or five days he is still persisting in his request, then let him be allowed to come in, and remain in the guest quarters for a few days. After that he should be in the quarters of the novices, where they work and eat and sleep. And to them should be assigned a senior monk who has the gift of winning souls, and he should pay them the closest attention. His care must be to find out whether the newcomer sincerely seeks God, whether he is earnest at the Work of God, in obedience and under severe words. All the things that are hard and repugnant to nature in the way to God are to be expounded to him.

Apr. 11
Aug. 11
Dec. 11

If he promises to persevere in his intention to remain, after two months have passed, this Rule is to be read to him from beginning to end, and he is to be told, 'This is the law under which you are asking to live. If you can keep it, come in; if however you cannot, freely depart.' If he still stands his ground, then he is to be led to the above-mentioned novices' quarters, and once again his patience under all kinds of trials is to be put to the test. After the passing of another six months, the Rule is to be read to him so that he may know what he

[1] I Jn 4:1

is entering on. If he still remains, after four months the same Rule is to be read to him again. Then, if, having thought the matter over carefully, he promises to keep all the rules, and to obey all the orders given him, he should be admitted into the community. He must, however, realise that it is set down in the law of the Rule that from that day onward he may not leave the monastery, nor cast off from his neck the yoke of the Rule which it was open to him during all this lengthy deliberation to decline or to undertake.

Apr. 12 Aug. 12 Dec. 12 The one who is to be accepted into the community must promise in the oratory in the presence of all, stability, conversion of life and obedience. He is to do this before God and all his saints, so that if he subsequently behaves otherwise, he will know that he merits condemnation by him whom he mocks. With regard to this promise he must write a petition, calling on the names of the saints whose relics are there, and in the name of the Abbot who is present. This petition he should write with his own hand or, if he is illiterate, it must be written by another whom he has asked, and the novice must make his sign on it. And he should place it with his own hand on the altar. When he has done so, the novice himself straightway intones this verse, *Accept me Lord according to your word, and I shall live, and you will not disappoint me in my hope* [2] The whole community repeats this verse three times, adding *Glory be to the Father* at the end. Then the brother novice prostrates himself at the feet of each of the brethren, asking their prayers. Then from that day onwards he is to be reckoned among the community. If he has any pos-

---

[2] Ps 118:116

sessions, he must either previously give them to the poor, or by means of a formal donation give them to the monastery, keeping for himself nothing at all, since he realises that from that day he will have no power even over his own body. At once then in the oratory, let him be stripped of his own clothes which he is wearing, and reclothed in those of the monastery. The clothes, however, which have been taken from him must be placed in the wardrobe, and kept there, so that if at some later time he should agree to the suggestion of the devil that he should leave the monastery (which God forbid), he can be stripped of the clothing of the monastery before being sent away. He does not, however, get back the petition which the Abbot took off the altar, but it is kept in the monastery.

The Admission, Training and Profession of new Brethren

1 The first reaction to the newcomer who knocks at the monastery door is one of discouragement. He is not let in at all. He will receive a kindly answer provided that he does not say that he wants to come in permanently. If he does, then it will take him days to get as far as the guest-house. Is this attitude relevant to modern times? It seems that we have to tread more lightly. For in a world in which many are discouraged in spiritual matters and groping uncertainly after spiritual values, we have to avoid giving the impression that the monks don't care. St Benedict's motive was that it would be better for the young man to realise from the start that the monastery was not a place to escape to, nor suitable for weaklings. It was a kind of answer which that age could interpret. The need for discretion about new admissions is still there, but we have to go at the business more intelligibly.

2 After a brief stay in the guest-house the postulant graduates to the noviciate, a part of the house reserved for newcomers. He will not mix overmuch with the community, for there he will study, eat and sleep; but he will be present at the common prayer and take his part in the work of the house. The negative attitude to his admittance is changed to a positive one. He will be in the charge of a brother who has *the gift of winning souls*, who will study his character and needs. He is not to be enticed; the hardships of the way before him will be explained; the Rule and its considerable demands will be read to him; yet also the promises that are contained in this way of life will be expounded to him. On his side, he will have a year to make up his mind whether it is what he wants. On the community's side he will be judged by three tests:

(i) Is he earnest at the Work of God? Prayer is the charism of the monk. He who is not interested should not proceed

(ii) At obedience? This is an essential element in the monastic life. If he is not disposed for it, he cannot become a monk

(iii) At severe words, that is, in the acceptance of trials? For without steadfastness he will make a sorry business of becoming a monk.

3 *Whether he sincerely seeks God:* The expression is found in Psalm 27:8,9 (Jerusalem Bible).

My heart has said of you: Seek his face.
Lord I do seek your face; do not hide your face from me.

The Rule does not treat explicitly of mysticism, nor of desiring the gift of contemplation. What was considered, at any rate at this stage, was: Does he sincerely seek (to do the Will of) God, to live in a response to his commandments? For then, as the Prologue says, he will find God close to him. '*And before you call on me, I shall say to you, "Here I am*!" '

4 The deep religious significance of the final acceptance is indicated by its taking place in the oratory '*before God and all his Saints*' (especially those represented by their relics preserved in the monastery).

The taking of vows has a double effect. On the one hand the Church, acknowledging these vows, sees the monk's life as governed in the future by the rules of the fraternity he has joined and accords him the special position of a dedicated person in her society. On the other hand, interiorly, the vows are solemn promises by which he binds himself to God's service, setting up a permanent spiritual pattern for all the days of his life. Thus the taking of vows constitutes the making of the monk. In the Rule they are three:

(i) *Stability:* By this vow a man undertook to remain constant in his profession and in that particular family for all his days. In exchange he acquired a new family responsible for caring for him

(ii) *Obedience:* Permanence in community would be useless and worse, without the practice of obedience; this meant obedience to the Rule and its interpretation by the Abbot. For our times there are also the interpretations given by constitutions

(iii) *Conversion of Life:* This is understood as the continuous practice of turning away from worldly ways and habits, and to the fulfilment of the Gospel precepts, understood in the monastic setting. This implies the giving up of marriage, of possessions, of ambitions, of wealthy living, and on the positive side, a life of prayer and fraternal community.

5 There are four points in the ceremony of profession:

(i) The candidate reads his vows and signs them. He lays them on the altar as a sign of oblation

(ii) He sings the verse *Accept me O Lord.* The significance of this verse may be brought out by paraphrasing it thus: Accept, O Lord, this oblation of all my days as made over to your service; I make it conscious of my weakness, but trusting in your word, and your promise that I may find new life in you; the trust that is placed in you is never overthrown.

As the vows represent a dying to self-will, so the expectation expressed is to share in the Risen Life of Christ (*I shall live*).

The community who have all gone this way themselves support his prayer by singing the verse after him. It is for them an act of renewal

(iii) Prostrating himself before each of the community and receiving the prayer of each, the new monk is accepted into the fraternity

(iv) His clothes are changed for those of the monastery. He is no longer his own man.

Chapter LIX The Sons of the Rich or the Poor who are offered

Apr. 13 Aug. 13 Dec. 13 If it happens that a nobleman offers his son to God as a monk, and the child is still of tender age, the parents should make out the petition of which we have spoken. They should wrap this petition and the boy's hand together with the Mass offering in the altar cloth and offer him in that way. As for his property, they must in the same petition promise under oath that on no occasion will they ever give him anything either themselves or through an agent or by any other means, nor will they afford him any opportunity for possessing anything. However, if they are unwilling to do this, and want to have the merit of giving something as an alms to the monastery, they should make a donation to the monastery of whatever they want to give; they may reserve the income of it to themselves if they wish. Thus will be blocked every way by which expectation might remain to deceive the child and (God forbid), lead him to destruction, as we have learnt by experience.

And poorer people may follow the same procedure. As for those who possess nothing at all, they may simply make the petition and offer their son with the Mass offering in the presence of witnesses.

The Oblation of a Child

What seems to us a surprising overlooking of human rights did not present any such problem to St Benedict. This was partly because in those days parents planned their children's lives to a far greater degree than in our own. But perhaps even more to the point was the story in Scripture of Anna making over her new-born child to the Lord:

'This is the child I prayed for, and Yahweh granted me what I asked him. Now I make him over to Yahweh for the whole of this life. He is made over to Yahweh.[1]

The men of those days did not see any reason why this scriptural example should not be repeated. Nor why parents who baptised their children should not consecrate them further to God. Our own greatly developed sense of human rights rules out all such transactions. For us it is clear that life is indeed a gift from God and (on their level) from parents, but that each individual has to decide how he will use it.

---

[1] I S 1:27–8 (Jerusalem Bible)

Chapter LX Priests who may want to live in the Monastery

Apr. 14 Aug. 14 Dec. 14 If anyone of the rank of priest asks to be taken into the monastery, this should not be granted him too quickly. If, however, he is very persistent in his request, he must understand that he will have to observe the full discipline of the Rule, and that no relaxation will be made for him, as the Scripture says, 'Friend, for what purpose have you come?'[1] Nevertheless it may be granted him to stand next to the Abbot, to pronounce blessings, and to celebrate Mass, provided the Abbot gives permission. Otherwise he must not take any privilege for granted, knowing that he is subject to the discipline of the Rule, and should give greater proofs of humility to all. Moreover, in the event of some appointment or other monastic business coming up for consideration, he must keep the position in community which goes with the date of his entry into the monastery, and not the one granted him out of reverence for the priesthood.

If any clerics should show the same desire to join the monastery, they should be placed in a slightly advanced position in community, and they, too, must promise observance of the Rule and stability.

The Admission of a Priest

1 The monk saw his life as very different from that of the priest. The latter was a privileged person, trained to minister to the people of God, a person to be honoured by them. The monk had given

[1] Mt 26:50

up whatever status he may have had in the world, whatever prospects he might have had of preferment, and even his own freedom of action. He sought only to fulfil all the Gospel precepts in his own life, with a rule to guide him and a community of brethren to sustain him. Why then should a priest knock on a monastery door? Hence the instruction that his motives should be well scrutinised before admittance was granted.

2 Once he was admitted, the respect due to his priesthood would not be forgotten. His consecration was not a matter of indifference in the household of God. But the privileges which should in all seemliness follow from his sacerdotal status are distinguished from claims to preferment to office, and these are not accepted.

3 *Friend, for what purpose have you come*? The words are apt—*if* read without reference to the context. To make use of a few words of Scripture, apt in themselves, to illustrate some point, came naturally enough to men who were so soaked in Scripture that its words clothed their thoughts unbidden.

Chapter LXI How Pilgrim Monks are to be received

Apr. 15 Aug. 15 Dec. 15 If a pilgrim monk should arrive from some far-off locality, and want to live as a guest in the monastery, and be content with the customs that he finds there, and not disturb the community by making special demands, but be quite content with what he finds, then let him be accepted for as long as he desires. And if indeed with humble charity he reasonably criticises or points some things out, the Abbot should consider the matter carefully. For it may be that the Lord has sent him for this very purpose. And if later on he wants to settle down permanently, this desire is not to be refused, especially as his way of life could be well known during his time as a guest.

Apr. 16 Aug. 16 Dec. 16 If on the other hand during that time, he should be found demanding or a man of bad habits, not only should he not be allowed to join the community, but he should be frankly told to go away, for fear that others should be corrupted by his unhappy condition.

If, however, he is not the kind which deserves dismissal, not only should he be admitted to the community if he so petitions, but he should be persuaded to stay so that others may be instructed by his example, and because it is the one Lord we serve in every place, and the one King for whom the battle is fought. Indeed if the Abbot sees him to be of sufficient virtue, he may place him in a somewhat higher position. In fact the Abbot may assign a more honourable position than that due to the day of entry not only to a monk, but to one coming from the above-mentioned ranks of priests or clerics, if he recognises that their way of life is worthy of such treatment. The Abbot, however, must take care never to accept permanently a monk from another known monastery without either the agreement of his Abbot or a letter of recommendation, since it is written, 'Do not to another what you would not want done to yourself.'[1]

The Admission of one already a Monk

1 St Benedict did not like the wandering type of monk (Ch. I) who lacked stability. His whole house was built on the principle of stability, and to achieve it he shows himself by turns, administrator, organiser, law-maker, disciplinarian, teacher. These human qualities are uplifted by the spirituality of the saint. But there is something else: an eager charismatic quality. He shows himself alert at all times for a new encounter with the Lord. Hence his mind is not blinkered: the pilgrim monk will be received not as a mere stranger, but as a brother; he may even be God's messenger. But discernment is necessary. Unlike other guests the brother is received into community and may stay as long as he wishes. But soon it will be noticed whether he has humility and is content with the fare he finds. Does he bring the peace of the Lord with him? Or alternatively, is he a critical man, difficult to satisfy, with fixed standards for his own comfort and nourishment?

If he turns out to be a good man, versed in the ways of the Lord, then (thinks St Benedict) maybe the Lord has sent him with a special message, and we should listen for it. It is basic to be able to recognise the Lord in the persons we meet; this calls for openness of spirit, and humility, and absence of bias. The community should not be so inward-looking, or so convinced that the visitor 'has not got our spirit' that they are unable to accept a new insight. There is an American story of a poor man who complained to the Lord that he could never gain admittance into a certain church, of which the congregation consisted of persons of a certain status in society. But the Lord consoled him, saying, 'Well, I never can get in there

---

[1] Tb 4:16

myself.' The author of the Rule for monks shows a humble attitude in thinking that he may receive some new insight, not from a celestial vision, but through the person of some stranger monk.

2 *Corrupted by his unhappy condition* (ejus miseria): How much experience underlay the choice of that word *miseria*, with its recognition of the unhappiness, and so bad influence of the fallen monk. Certain it is that to be bound by vow to seek God with constant effort and yet simultaneously to have forsaken the quest, is to have to carry round a 'dis-eased' heart in both senses of the word.

3 *It is one Lord we serve in every place:* There is here again something we might call charismatic in this perception that the Lord is lord of all, and is being served in every place. We tend to be confined in our thinking, so that we think too exclusively in terms of the contribution we make ourselves, or through our own institution or style of service. But God's picture is surely different: he receives, accepts and is honoured by services from so many sources. And this thought should make us conscious of a oneness in him, that adds greatly to Christian joy.

Chapter LXII The Priests of the Monastery

If an Abbot wishes to have a priest or deacon ordained for his service, he should choose from his monks one who is fit to exercise the priesthood. He who is ordained, however, must beware of elation or pride and he should not take upon himself any work that has not been committed to him by the Abbot. Apr. 17 Aug. 17 Dec. 17

He should realise that he is all the more bound to submit to monastic discipline. Nor on account of his priesthood should he forget the obedience and the discipline of the Rule, but he should go forward more and more towards God.

Except when officiating at the altar, let him always keep the position corresponding to his entry into the monastery; unless the choice of the community and the will of the Abbot promote him to a higher station on account of the merit of his life. He should realise that he is bound by the rule laid down for deans and priors; if he presumes to behave otherwise, the judgement will be passed not on the priest but on the rebellion. If after frequent warnings he does not mend his ways, the Bishop also should be called in as a witness against him. If even so he does not amend and his faults are manifest, he must be expelled from the monastery—that is if his stubbornness is such that he will neither submit nor obey the Rule.

The Position of Priests in the Community

1 To have a priest among their number was an advantage to the community, since it meant that they did not have to go out to Mass or arrange for a priest to come in to attend to their needs. So St Benedict authorises the ordination of a priest from among the monks, and also of a deacon to assist him. The motive is the good of the community.

This leads to two characteristic thoughts: (1) the danger of the monk's becoming proud or elated, (2) the dynamic idea that the priesthood is a source of grace, by which *he should go forward more and more towards God.* The monastic life is never just a routine; as on a pilgrimage, the daily actions may be repetitive, but each brother is to be always moving towards his spiritual goal.

In later centuries, when monasteries became centres of pilgrimage, there was a great need for dispensing the sacraments. And so it became customary for all suitable monks to be ordained priest. A contributory cause was the growth in solemn offices. Eventually Canon Law required solemnly professed monks to go on to Holy Orders. This ruling has now been changed, and today a man who seeks the monastic state does not necessarily expect to be ordained, or feel the vocation for it.

2 *The rule laid down for deans and priors:* He may be moved to a higher position for *the merit of his life*, but, like these officials, if he is not edifying, he may be moved down again, cf. Ch. XXI, at the end.

3 *The Bishop should be called in:* The failure of a priest-monk is seen as more serious than that of an ordinary monk. Only after the Bishop has borne witness to the state of affairs, will the question of expulsion be considered.

Chapter LXIII The Order of the Community

The time of their entering monastic life, their personal merits, and the decision of the Abbot, shall decide the order which they keep in the monastery. Yet the Abbot must not upset the flock entrusted to him, nor should he make any unjust arrangement as though he were free to give orders as he pleases, for he must always bear in mind that he is going to have to render an account of all his decisions and actions. In the order, then, which he has laid down, or which they otherwise have among themselves, shall the brethren come to the kiss of peace, or to Communion, or intone a Psalm or occupy their place in choir. In no circumstances or places is age to decide order or have any bearing upon it, for the youthful Samuel and Daniel acted as judges over their elders. Therefore, with the exception of those whom, as we have said, the Abbot has promoted or degraded for definite reasons, the rest are to take their places according to the time of their coming to the monastery; for example one who has entered the monastery at the second hour is to know that he is junior to him who entered at the first, whatever his age or dignity. For the boys, however, all have the task of keeping order wherever they are. Apr. 18 Aug. 18 Dec. 18

Juniors, therefore, must show respect for their seniors, and seniors must love their juniors. In calling one another by name it is not allowed to any one to use the name alone: seniors should address their juniors with the title Brother; and juniors address their seniors as *Nonnus*, by which is signified the reverence due to a father. The Abbot, however, as he is believed to act in Apr. 19 Aug. 19 Dec. 19

the place of Christ should be called Lord and Abbot, not because he demands these titles, but for the honour and love of Christ. He himself must bear this in mind, and show himself worthy of such honour.

Whenever the brethren meet one another, the junior should seek a blessing of the elder. A younger monk should rise and offer the seat to an older one if he passes by, nor should he venture to sit down again, unless the older one tells him to, so that it may be as it is written, 'Forestall one another in paying honour.'[1]

Children and youths are to keep their places, in good order, in the oratory and at table. Out of doors also and anywhere at all they should be under supervision and discipline, until they reach an age that can understand.

The Order of the Community. Mutual Relations

1 The 'alternative society' of the monastery was based on the principle of essential equality in God's service (cf. Ch.II *We serve on equal terms. . .*), but it is not a mob without an order or manners. This chapter deals with both. The order was settled not by age, valuable service, talent or dignity (not even the priestly dignity constituted a right), but on a simple principle that in itself involved no merit: the hour in which the Lord called the brother to his service. The hour of his calling is the hour of the spiritual rebirth of each one. This was the only normal principle. Yet it could be modified by the Abbot if he saw good reason for a change. But the Abbot is threatened with the judgement of God if he disturbs the brethren unnecessarily. For we are all human, and it is human to belong to a society, not merely in a general way, but through one's niche in it.

2 *Samuel and Daniel:* From Scripture St Benedict concluded that God sometimes makes use of the young for special tasks; with all

---

[1] Rm 12:10

his insistence that the disciples' task is to listen (Prol., Ch. VI), he is conscious that God may speak through the young. Each man, he wrote in Ch. XL, *has his special gift from God*, and the young may be the recipients of special gifts. In this he thinks prophetically; it is not that the young are to be preferred as such, but that God sometimes chooses them as recipients of his action, and this is to be acknowledged by all.

3 The second half of the chapter deals with manners. For the Rule this had nothing to do with social class; it was not the prerogative of the better educated in the community. Good manners towards one another are a necessary substratum in the structure of the house of God. How shall we be ready to receive the divine courtesies if we have not learnt courtesy to one another? What follows is not a complete code of social manners, for such instructions are scattered throughout the Rule, but treats certain points more or less connected with the community's order.

4 *No one is allowed to use the name alone:* We think of this usage as implying intimacy and therefore love. And this is true. But there are other aspects, and certain pitfalls attendant on this natural custom. It can imply a distinction of tenderness. I may refer to John or Johnny (my pal) and to Br James (outside my circle). It may also imply a lack of reverence towards another, and may in fact combine too easily with uncomplimentary adjectives (Old so-and-so!). What St Benedict seeks is not stiffness, but a showing of equal esteem and charity. And in a sense that is what manners are about.

5 *Nonnus:* It was 'a familiar and affectionate title addressed to persons who although not in the ranks of the ecclesiastical hierarchy properly so called are nevertheless worthy of a particular regard: monks, nuns, clerics, ascetics, virgins, widows, the aged' (J. M. Henssens). Obsolete for men, it survives in the word 'nun'.

6 *Called Lord and Abbot:* Among the monks of the Egyptian deserts the title *Abba* was applied to one who was revered for wisdom and holiness; it was thus a recognition of spiritual maturity. In the Rule and generally at this period it meant simply the Father of a monastic family. In the Middle Ages, when all Abbots were priests, the Abbot was numbered among the higher clergy, becoming a prelate and often a local magnate by reason of the size of the monastic domains. Moreover, the word *Lord* acquired a feudal significance unknown to earlier ages. The Church conceded to him the marks of rank associated with a Bishop: ring and pectoral cross, and a limited use of the mitre (emblem of the high priesthood, Ex 28:4) and crozier (emblem of the pastor or shepherd, Ps. 22:4). Today, following Vatican II, the tendency is towards a simplification of these traditions. Usually an Abbot is the head of a monastic family, but occasionally monks receive the rank of titular Abbot.

7 The principle is laid down that the discipline of children concerns all. As man develops a new understanding of himself he develops a new understanding of the child. And so the meaning of the word discipline changes. The new meaning will imply an understanding of the laws and stages by which God meant his children to evolve, with the freedom and outreach that this implies. And this is the wisdom with which children need to be surrounded, and is therefore a concern for all.

Chapter LXIV The Institution of the Abbot

This principle must always be kept in mind in the institution of the Abbot: He should be appointed whom the united community chooses in the fear of God, or whom a smaller part of the community chooses with the sounder judgement. He who is to be appointed must be chosen on account of his virtuous life and wise teaching, even if he is the last in order in the community. So that even if (may it not happen!) the whole community should with one accord elect a person who will connive at their defects, and if these defects somehow become known to the Bishop to whose diocese the place belongs, and to the local abbots or Christians, they should put a stop to this plot of wicked men, and set a worthy steward over the household of God. And they should know that they will receive a good reward if they act with a pure intention and zeal for God, and that on the other hand it would be sinful to neglect their duty. Apr. 20 Aug. 20 Dec. 20

When he has been instituted, the Abbot should always bear in mind what a burden he has undertaken, and to whom he will have to render an account of his stewardship. He should know, too, that he ought to be of profit to his brethren rather than just preside over them. He ought, therefore, to be learned in the divine law, so that he may know it well, and that it may be for him a store whence he draws forth new things and old. He should be a chaste man, temperate and merciful. He should always prefer mercy to judgement,[1] that he may Apr. 21 Aug. 21 Dec. 21

[1] Jm 2:13

also obtain mercy. Let him hate sin, let him love the brethren.

In correcting he should act prudently, and not overdo it; for fear that as he tries too hard to get rid of the rust, the pot gets broken. Also he should always mistrust his own frailty and remember that the bruised reed is not to be broken. In saying these things, we do not imply that he should allow vices to flourish, but that he should eliminate them prudently and with charity, as seems best in each case, as we have already said. And it should be his aim to be loved rather than feared. Let him not be restless or anxious, not over-demanding and obstinate, not a perfectionist or full of suspicion, or he will never have any peace. In giving his instructions he should have forethought and consideration; and whether the instructions which he gives concern God's affairs or temporal ones, let him be discerning and moderate, bearing in mind the discretion of holy Jacob who said, 'If I cause my flocks to be overdriven, they will all die in one day.'[2]

Taking to heart therefore these and other examples of discretion, the mother of virtues, he should so regulate everything that the strong may desire to carry more, and the weak are not afraid.

And, especially, he must in every respect keep this present Rule so that having fulfilled his ministry well, he may hear from the Lord the same words as that good servant who gave his fellow servants wheat in due season, 'Truly I say to you, he will place him over everything he owns.'[3]

---

[2] Gn 33:13 [3] Mt 24:47

How the Abbot receives his Office. His Stewardship

1 The community had a right to a say in the choice of their superior and spiritual leader. This is recognised in the holding of an election. But the election was not necessarily decisive. The appointment was made by the Bishop, assisted it seems by the local Abbots (cf. Ch.LXV: The Prior of the Monastery). Even local Christians are thought of as being concerned with the good estate of their monastery. If then the monks fall into the temptation of electing one who from weakness or worse would be unable to keep up the standards of monastic life and discipline, the Rule urges the Bishop to exercise his responsibility, set the unworthy choice aside and appoint another who has less support in votes but is more worthy of confidence.

Today the right of confirmation of an abbatial election is mostly held by the president of the monastic congregation to which the monastery belongs; and he receives this authority through constitutions approved by the Holy See.

2 After the election came the *Ordinatio* of the Abbot. As it did not confer sacramental orders, it is translated as *Institution* here. In this solemn ceremony the Bishop prayed that the Holy Spirit might endow the Abbot with the virtues and gifts appropriate to his position as Father and leader of his community. And thereafter the Church recognised him as ordained or instituted as Abbot.

3 *A worthy steward over the household of God:* The expression 'household of God' (Latin: *Domus Dei*) comes from 1 Tim 3, 14–15 where it describes 'the church of the living God, the pillar and bulwark of the truth'. The Rule uses it three times. Here and in Ch XXXI, it has reference to the care of those who form this spiritual house. In Ch LIII it seems to refer rather to the material building whose upkeep and arrangements are to be *wisely cared for* by wise men. Though it uses quite different terms the Prologue is also occupied with the thought of the monk as a dweller in God's house (*habitator tabernaculi eius*).

4 The lines of advice addressed to the newly elected Abbot are truly golden; they are marked, too, by a greater gentleness than was apparent in Ch II.

When Lord Mansfield said to Dr Samuel Johnson, 'Severity is

not the way to govern boys or men,' the latter replied, 'Nay, it is the way to govern them; I know not if it is the way to mend them.' The distinction was ever present to St Benedict. His preoccupations were with healing souls, who all suffer from wounds of sin, and with leading them onwards to God, the source of all love. He tries to inculcate moderation not severity, nor slackness. He underlines that the Abbot must show himself as lovable—not for his own sake, for that would be a disorientation, but in order that he may lead men to God.

5 *He must keep this present rule*, both himself as one of the brethren and in his office as head of the monastery. But the latitude left to him is vast. He will understand that the Rule contains three types of directives: doctrinal, juridical and observances. And of the last category, almost all observances are left to be tempered by the Abbot's judgement. St Benedict does not rely on the letter of what he has written; the Abbot has to understand it more deeply than that.

Chapter LXV The Prior of the Monastery

It happens fairly often that serious scandals occur in monasteries because of the appointment of a Prior; for there are those who, swelling up with an evil spirit of pride, consider themselves second abbots, act like tyrants and nourish scandals and quarrels in the community. This happens especially in places where the Prior is appointed by the same Bishop or by the same abbots as appoint the Abbot of the monastery. It is easy to see how unwise this is: for from the very beginning of his appointment the Prior is given grounds for waxing proud, since his thoughts suggest to him that he is exempt from the Abbot's authority, because 'You have been appointed by the same persons as the Abbot.' Hence arise envy, quarrels, detraction, rivalries, dissensions and disorders; for while the Abbot and Prior are in opposition to each other, of necessity their own souls are endangered by this quarrelling, and also those under their authority seeking favour from one side or the other head for perdition. The evils arising from such a dangerous state of affairs are due primarily to those who have been the originators of such a disorder. Apr. 22 Aug. 22 Sept. 22

For this reason we think it expedient for the preservation of peace and charity that the making of appointments in the monastery should depend on the Abbot's judgement and, if it is possible, that all the business of the monastery should be carried on through deans, under the control of the Abbot, as we have already laid down. Thus no one may wax proud over what is committed to many. Apr. 23 Aug. 23 Dec. 23

If, however, local conditions require it, or the community makes a reasonable and humble request, and the Abbot judges it to be expedient, then the Abbot himself should appoint as his Prior whomsoever he chooses after taking the advice of God-fearing brethren. For his part the Prior is to perform respectfully whatever functions the Abbot lays upon him, and to do nothing contrary to his will or arrangements. For inasmuch as he has been placed over others, he should the more carefully keep the precepts of the Rule. If it should turn out that the Prior has serious faults or, deceived by vanity, acts arrogantly, or it turns out that he is a belittler of the Holy Rule, he should be verbally rebuked up to four times; if he does not then change his ways, he should be punished according to the disciplinary code. If, however, he does not amend even so, then he must be deposed from his office as Prior, and another who is suitable for it be put in his place. And if afterwards he does not live quietly and obediently among the community, he should even be expelled from the monastery.

The Abbot should, however, bear in mind the account he must render to God for all his decisions, for fear that the flame of jealousy or evil zeal burn in his soul.

The Prior of the Monastery

1 This chapter is unlike any other in the Rule. The others, particularly those that concern the compacting together of the principal personnel of the house of God, are calm, solid, three-dimensional. But this one opens with an explosion: it is not so much a regulation of the Prior's office as almost a statement of disapproval of it altogether. Nor are any specific duties assigned to this important office; and the same negative attitude is reflected throughout the Rule.

2 We may find the explanation of this strong prejudice in the parallel legislation in the *Rule of the Master*. This document was once thought to be later than St Benedict, but now scholars place it earlier.

According to this Rule the monastery normally has no Prior, but provides that the Abbot when dying shall designate his successor, who will then be appointed by the Bishop. But, what if, after this, the Abbot does not die but recovers? Then the appointed one must wait his day, and in the interval becomes a kind of Prior, with right of succession:

> For on account of his good observance and his extreme humility God has chosen him, and the Abbot consented; the Bishop has appointed him, and from this day forward let him sit beside the Abbot as one deputed to become a spiritual Caesar.[1]

Evidently St Benedict did not want a 'spiritual Caesar' in his monastery; but he manages to reach the conclusion that in certain circumstances and with due safeguards, it may be right to appoint a Prior; but he adds some more warnings on the subject.

3 In fact history has judged in the main that St Benedict's fears were exaggerated, and that a second-in-command is an invaluable, perhaps indispensable official in the monastery. Canon Law at present requires every religious house to have one person to act as deputy for the superior as occasion and custom may require.

[1]Rule of the Master, Ch. 93

Chapter LXVI The Doorkeepers of the Monastery

Apr. 24
Aug. 24
Dec. 24

At the gate of the monastery a wise old man is to be posted, one capable of receiving a message and giving a reply, and whose maturity guarantees that he will not wander round. This doorkeeper should have a cell near the gate, so that persons who arrive may always find someone at hand to give them a reply. As soon as anyone knocks, or a poor man calls out, he should answer 'Thanks be to God' or 'God bless you.' Then with all the gentleness that comes from the fear of God, he should speedily and with the warmth of charity attend to the enquirer.

If the gatekeeper needs it, he should have a younger brother to help him.

If it is possible the monastery should be organised so that all its needs, that is to say things such as water, a mill, a garden, various crafts, may be met within its premises, so that the monks have no need to wander round outside it, for that does not profit their souls at all.

This Rule we wish to be read frequently in the community, so that none of the brethren may plead ignorance of it.

The Doorkeeper. The Premises

1 The three top officials and the deans have received the attention of a chapter each. The last word, as if one were halting at the door before leaving the premises, goes to the doorkeeper. Rightly he is seen as a public relations officer, for many outsiders will form their opinion of the monastery from his behaviour. This is even more true today of the person who takes telephone messages. An old man is suitable, but any old fool will not do. He must be wise and kind: wise enough to handle the persons who arrive, kindly enough to treat the poorest of them with consideration.

2 He must be on the spot and answer the knock or the door-bell promptly. It is remarkable how the details of all that can go wrong or cause irritation are foreseen. But the thought that he must not wander about prompts another thought: that wandering about outside the monastery will not be good for anybody. A short list follows of what the monastery should if possible contain; it is a very modest one and refers to items essential for daily life: water, the mill for bread, a garden for vegetables, and the various buildings for arts and crafts. Nothing of wide fields or extensive domains. Compared to St Basil's conception of a monastery with a church, hostel and hospital with staff of doctors and male nurses, shelter for travellers, poor people and the sick, including lepers, the requirements are modest indeed (cf. Marrou. *The Christian Centuries*, p. 238).

From the last sentence: This Rule we wish to be read, *the commentators conclude that this was the end of the Rule as planned. The seven chapters that follow are in the nature of appendices.*

Appendix

Chapter LXVII Brethren sent on a Journey

Brethren who are being sent on a journey are to commend themselves to the prayers of all the brethren and of the Abbot; and in the final prayer of the Work of God there should be a commemoration of all who are absent. When brethren return from a journey, at all the canonical hours of the day on which they return, they should lie prostrate on the floor of the oratory, as the Work of God comes to an end, and ask for the prayers of all,[1] for any faults that may have overtaken them on their journey, such as the sight or hearing of an evil thing or idle chatter. No one should venture to tell another anything he may have seen or heard while outside the monastery, for that does much harm. But if anyone does this he must undergo punishment according to the Rule. The same thing applies to anyone who dares to go out of the enclosure of the monastery, or to go anywhere, or do anything, although of small importance, without the approval of the Abbot.

Apr. 25
Aug. 25
Dec. 25

Rules for the Brethren who travel

1 An errand (Ch LI) is one thing, a journey another. It implies a break in one's normal routine and separation from the family. Also journeys were slow and reckoned as perilous. There were dangers of the road, and also (thinks St Benedict) dangers to the soul. Hence prayer is called for on departure for protection, during the journey for the absentees and in thanksgiving when the travellers return.

Our psychology is vastly different. We do not normally regard

---

[1] cf. Tb 11:7 (Vulg.)

a journey as perilous, nor even as a probable hazard to the soul. We often think it may do good to the traveller; we regard a relation of interesting happenings as normal, and in some cases edifying. Even allowing for the differences between monastic houses, we are differently conditioned about travel from our earliest days.

Yet it is just as true that we need that the Lord go with us and protect us on our journeys; that we gain by the loving prayers offered in our absence; that we owe thanksgiving to God on our safe return.

2 *To do anything . . without the approval of the Abbot:* The words suggest the ancient tradition of the guru: in this a man adhered to the master of his choice and followed his instructions and copied his example down to the smallest details. In fact it is intended as a general, though strong, protest against individualism. The need for maturity and personal wisdom is stressed in many places of the Rule, particularly when officials are to be chosen.

Chapter LXVIII If a Brother is set impossible Tasks

If it should happen that burdensome or impossible tasks are imposed on one of the brethren he should indeed accept the command of the one who so orders with complete calm and obedience, but if he sees that the weight of the burden quite exceeds the limits of his strength, he should quietly and at a suitable moment explain to his superior the reasons why he cannot do it, not in a proud way nor with the spirit of resistance, or contradiction. But if after his explanations the one in authority remains firm in requiring what he has ordered, the junior must understand that this is what is best for him, and let him lovingly trust in God's aid, and so obey.

Apr. 26
Aug. 26
Dec. 26

The Case of impossible Demands

The chapter was not written to encourage the making of harsh or impossible commands, which is against the spirit of the Rule.

It is as if St Benedict said, 'I have set down how superiors and juniors are to act to one another, but just one more point occurs to me. Situations can arise in which a person in authority asks—or seems to ask—altogether too much. What is to happen then?' And he gives to the one in this difficulty advice that will lead him to serenity and spiritual maturity. We are outside the realm of the legislator; it is the spiritual counsellor who speaks, and he speaks gently and lovingly saying, 'Do your best, rely on God, and you will see that he knows how to draw good things for you out of this situation.'

The advice is of special value also to the diffident man who underestimates his own ability and to the man faced with a grave situation. For one's own strength is not the real measure. 'Lord,' said

Gideon, 'how can I deliver Israel? Behold my clan is the weakest in Manasseh, and I am the least in my family.' And the Lord said to him, 'But I will be with you.'[1]

---

[1] Jg 6:15–16

Chapter LXIX That in the Monastery one must not defend Another

Let it be noted that in the monastery no monk may assume the right to defend or act as a kind of protector to another for any reason whatever, even if they are connected by a bond of blood-relationship. Monks must not presume to do this in any way, for from it may arise the possibility of very grave scandals. If anyone offends in this respect he must be sharply dealt with.

Apr. 27
Aug. 27
Dec. 27

Prohibition of personal Alliances

'Love', said the poet, 'is a many-splendour'd thing.' The form of love which concerns us here is the love among the brotherhood, a supernatural growth indeed but springing from human hearts with all their need to love and be loved, and purified by the pursuit of a greater charity. In these final chapters the Rule is concerned with the love of the brotherhood, the dangers to which it is exposed, and how to nourish it.

The danger alluded to briefly here is that human relationship or natural affinity may replace or distort the spiritual love that is called for; this may show itself in taking another under one's protection. St Benedict does not think it necessary to explain; nor is explanation necessary. We recognise the situation well enough.

It is not that we are forbidden to love one another in a warm and human way; nor that love has to be so generalised as to fall on no one in particular. We are nearer the mark if we think that love should fall on everyone in particular—nor is a monastic friendship a wrong thing; but it has to be purified of the You-are-for-me element which is so natural and normal in human love. It cannot be exclusive.

Chapter LXX That no one may hit Another

Apr. 28
Aug. 28
Dec. 28

All outbreaks of self-assertiveness are to be avoided in the monastery. We therefore lay down that no one is allowed to excommunicate or strike any of his brethren, unless the Abbot has given him authority to do so. 'Those who offend must be rebuked in the presence of all, so that the rest may be warned.'[1] Care, however, and supervision are to be shown by everyone with regard to the discipline of children up to fifteen years of age; yet with all moderation and good sense. With regard to those who are older than that, if anyone presumes to take action without the Abbot's instruction, or gets angry and behaves without discretion to the children also, he must submit to the discipline of the Rule, for it is written, 'Do not to another what you would not have done to yourself.'[2]

Prohibition of personal Attacks

If in Ch. LXIX it is forbidden to defend or form a personal alliance with another, here it is forbidden to condemn on one's own authority. Nor is this injunction remote from reality. For condemnation of another can take place in a man's heart, affecting his openness, his courtesy, his fraternal relationship with another. This can happen all too easily where the precept of asking forgiveness is not observed. Perhaps he who in a fit of temper strikes another does less harm than he who in cold blood keeps him excluded from fellowship.

In Ch. XXXVII the protective quality of the Rule, where the weak are concerned, was underlined. These lines give further emphasis to this aspect. In every society someone is liable to suffer.

---

[1] 1 Tm 5:20 [2] Tb 4:16

Chapter LXXI That the Brethren obey one Another

The goodness of obedience is not to be shown only through obedience to the Abbot, but the brethren should also all obey each other also, in the knowledge that by this path of obedience they will draw nearer God. The commands of the Abbot or of the superiors appointed by him must come first and we do not allow personal demands to be attended to before them; but otherwise all the younger monks should obey the older ones with all love and care. And if anyone is found to be contentious, he should be corrected. And if, for any reason at all, a brother is corrected in any way by the Abbot or by an elder, or if he perceives that the feelings of any elder have been roused to anger against him, even slightly, he should at once and without delay prostrate himself at his feet and lie there in sign of reparation until the rift is healed by a blessing. If anyone is too proud to do this, he must either undergo corporal punishment or, if he is contumacious, he must be put out of the monastery.

Apr. 29
Aug. 29
Dec. 29

Mutual Obedience

The opening words, *the goodness of obedience (obedientiae bonum)*, imply that obedience is not conceived as a negative, a restriction, but as something positive and profitable, a fruit of the Spirit, always capable of growth. Nor do virtues exist side by side in separate boxes: obedience is made alive through charity. Hence it has a horizontal development towards one's brethren. For where love grows, there grows also a willingness to oblige, and one comes to see another's need as an imperative. Much is written nowadays about 'availability' to others; this means for a brother that, within the framework of order, he is ever at the disposal of others.

And so when there is discord, it is imperative that it be eliminated at once. For individual discord troubles the peace of the house of God. It concerns all since 'peace is indivisible', flowing through all or disturbed in all. To understand this teaching one must recognise the extent to which the members of the community saw themselves as forming one body in Christ.

Hence it was not only a principle but also a rule that in cases of discord one must ask forgiveness of the other. This is not a rule that becomes dated. It is difficult in all ages.

Chapter LXXII On the good Zeal which Monks ought to have

As there is an evil zeal rooted in bitterness which separates from God and leads to hell, so there is a good zeal which separates from vice and leads to God and to eternal life. This, therefore, is the zeal which monks should practise with the most ardent love; in other words, they should forestall one another in paying honour.[1] They should with the greatest patience make allowance for one another's weaknesses, whether physical or moral. They should rival one another in practising obedience. No one should pursue what he thinks advantageous for himself, but rather what seems best for another. They should labour with chaste love at the charity of the brotherhood. They should fear God. They should love their Abbot with sincere and humble charity. They should prefer nothing whatever to Christ. Apr. 30 Aug. 30 Dec. 30

May he bring us all alike to life everlasting.

The Meaning of True Zeal

1 As he concludes his Rule St Benedict lays down the supreme principle: It is love that counts (cf. St John of the Cross: 'At the end of life the examination will be about love'). So this chapter applies this principle to all the circumstances of life. The zeal for the monastic observance, behaviour towards those with whom we live, decisions on a course to be followed—all are weighed in this scale, as we hope that all *will bring us to life everlasting*.

2 *They should labour at the charity of the brotherhood:* It is not club life, but the building of a spiritual edifice through love. Ordinary

[1] Rm 12:10

good will is not adequate, nor does a pleasant and tolerant disposition suffice. To learn to build that portion of the Mystical Body of Christ which is the community involves a man in labour, the coming to see his brethren as Christ sees them, and so to learn to love them warmly, helpfully but not possessively, even as Christ loved all whom he encountered.

3 *They make allowance for one another's weaknesses*, each man remembering that his own weaknesses (the weight of which on others he does not know) are being allowed for by the generosity of others.

4 The Rule is fundamentally a system of relationships—vertical and horizontal. The monastic life is unprofitable, even unworkable, unless it is understood as a means of promoting union with God and fraternity among men. This final chapter of the Rule, brief as always, underlines this heavily.

Epilogue

Chapter LXXIII That the whole Keeping of Justice[1] is not covered by this Rule

We have written this Rule so that by following it in monasteries, we may to some extent show that we lead blameless lives and possess a beginning of the monastic way of life. In addition there are for him who would hasten to the perfection of the monastic way the doctrines of the holy Fathers, which, if a man keeps them, will lead him to the height of perfection. For is not every page of the Old or New Testament, every word of the Divine Author, a most direct rule for our human life? Does not every book of the Catholic Fathers proclaim that we should make our way by the most direct path to our Creator. There are also the *Conferences*, and *Institutes*, and the *Lives of the Fathers*, and the *Rule* of our holy Father Basil. What are these works but aids to the attainment of virtue for good-living and obedient monks? But to us who are slothful, who live badly and who are negligent, they bring a blush of shame. Whoever you are, then, who are hurrying forward to your heavenly fatherland, do you with Christ's help fulfil this little Rule written for beginners; and then you will come at the end, under God's protection, to those heights of learning and virtue which we have mentioned above.

May 1
Aug. 31
Dec. 31

The Limitations of this Rule

No new doctrines or observances are added, but three points are

[1] Cf. Mt 3:15

made: the scope of the Rule is defined, the author points to what he considers more advanced reading, and there is a final word of encouragement.

1 The scope of the Rule, asserts the author, is to be a beginner's manual. Hence there is no expounding of mystical doctrine, no requirement of heroic asceticism, just solid instruction, with many references to human defects, warnings against pitfalls for the unwary, provision for correction. The laying of a solid foundation is not as easy as it sounds: St Benedict never mistakes the beginner's good intentions or spiritual sensations for the actual acquisition of virtue; and the Rule is such that this kind of mistake could not be made for long. Nor does he suggest that the monk will find all that his soul needs in the observances he lays down. On the contrary he knows that each will *have his own gift from God* (Ch. XL), enabling him to pray more, fast more, or make greater strides in whatever direction grace leads him. He knows also that it is in human nature to fall down on the way. For this, too, he provides without undue lamentation. The house of God will contain those who run fast in the way of God's commandments (Prologue), those who walk slowly, and those who have somehow gone off the track. He endeavours to provide for all, and is content to say, *This Rule is a small beginning*, enough to justify the name of monk.

2 He expects his monk to learn more from other sources, especially the Books of *divine authorship*, the Old and New Testaments. God speaks through the living word of Scripture.

He cites also the *Conferences* and *Institutes* of the Fathers. These are presumably the works of John Cassian, Abbot at Marseilles (written 415–429), for Cassian was the bridge through whom the customs of Eastern Monasticism came to be studied in the West. He has in fact taken a great deal from Cassian, refashioning it for his purposes. 'Benedict regarded his Rule as a framework to be filled in by the teaching of other writers, and especially Cassian. . . Almost everywhere the Rule went, Cassian went with it.'[2]

He cites, too, the ancient Fathers, and concludes that by comparison, his own generation were unequal to them and should think of themselves as *slothful and negligent*. It is a sentiment that St Benedict's descendants may ponder in relation to his own precepts. But if it is not easy to say, 'Thus it is with me,' it is even more

[2] Owen Chadwick, *John Cassian* (2nd Edition), pp. 154, 156

inexpedient to say 'Thus it is with us,' and the sentiment is not breathed over loudly in modern writings. It is surely true in the West that most of us live more affluently than our forefathers; that the perfection of common life is relatively rare in a generation who have been brought up as individualists to a man, that the attainment of full spiritual union in community through open confession of fault (Ch. XLVI) is a doctrine calling for rediscovery.

3 St Basil (330–79): His work was not a parallel document to that of St Benedict. St Basil was accustomed to give answers to questions asked him about the monastic life. These answers grew into a large body of teaching known as the Rules of St Basil. St Benedict expected his monks to be acquainted with them; this may explain the summary nature of his remarks on children, for St Basil offers enlightened treatment on the instruction of the young.

The Lives of the Fathers: to which we may add the lives of some of St Benedict's monastic descendants.

4 And lastly a word of encouragement. The Prologue was addressed to Whoever-you-are, and he, having embraced the Holy Rule, reappears at the end in words that echo the Prologue: *Whoever-you-are hurrying forward to your heavenly fatherland.* So he is encouraged to think that if he begins right and perseveres he will also have some savour of the heavenly fatherland while here below. *You will come*, he is assured, *with time to the heights.* These heights have been alluded to briefly at the end of the Prologue and again at the end of Ch. VII: So the Rule ends with a promise to anyone who gives himself to the monastic life with the simplicity and sincerity which are the guarantees of its fruits.